Dedicated to Neville and Doreen Lawrence
whose courage following the death of their son Stephen
woke the nation

TRUE
COLOURS

Attitudes to multiculturalism and the role of the government

Yasmin Alibhai-Brown

INSTITUTE FOR PUBLIC POLICY RESEARCH

30-32 Southampton St
London WC2E 7RA
Tel: 0171 470 6100
Fax: 0171 470 6111
ippr@easynet.co.uk
www.ippr.org.uk
Registered charity 800065

The Institute for Public Policy Research is an independent charity whose purpose is to contribute to public understanding of social, economic and political questions through research, discussion and publication. It was established in 1988 by leading figures in the academic, business and trade-union communities to provide an alternative to the free market think tanks.

IPPR's research agenda reflects the challenges facing Britain and Europe. Current programmes cover the areas of economic and industrial policy, Europe, governmental reform, human rights, defence, social policy, the environment and media issues.

Besides its programme of research and publication, IPPR also provides a forum for political and trade union leaders, academic experts and those from business, finance, government and the media, to meet and discuss issues of common concern.

Production & design by **EMPHASIS**
ISBN 1 86030 083 9
© IPPR 1999
Printed and bound in Great Britain by Biddles Ltd, Guildford and King's Lynn

Contents

Acknowledgements
About the author
Terminology

Acknowledgements

I am indebted to Sarah Spencer for suggesting the idea for this report and for all the invaluable help, advice and support she has given me and the project. Many of my colleagues at the IPPR have also contributed informally and formally to this report. My thanks to the funders: the Lord Ashdown Charitable Trust, the Churches Commission for Racial Justice, the Barrow Cadbury Trust and the Forbes Trust. Richard Stone, Director of the Ashdown Trust generously provided additional funds for the two surveys on attitudes which added an important dimension to the report. Pardeep Gill and Clare Ettinghausen were my very efficient assistants for some parts of the project. I am also indebted to my advisory board and all the people I interviewed and consulted in Britain, Canada, the Netherlands and Berlin.

About the author

Yasmin Alibhai-Brown is a part-time research fellow at the IPPR working with the human rights team. She also writes for *The Guardian*, *New Statesman*, is a columnist for *The Independent* and frequently broadcasts on radio and television. She is the author of several books on race and other matters. She is a member of the Home Office Race Forum and advises various institutions on these issues. Her last book, *No Place Like Home* was an autobiographical account of her life as an Asian in Uganda and subsequently here in the UK. She has been awarded a journalist's fellowship by the Rowntree Foundation and will be writing a book on mixed-race Britons later in 1999.

Terminology

The terminology to describe diverse British populations is fraught with difficulties as terms are changing all the time to represent new realities. We have settled for ethnic communities, black and Asian Britons as our preferred terms. At certain key points we have been obliged to use ethnic minorities or ethnic minority communities or ethnic minority populations, but as is discussed in the report, these may not be suitable in the changing landscapes of the future. We have used Britain and the United Kingdom interchangeably although these are seen as distinct by some people.

1. Introduction

As the Tebbit 'cricket test' and the Stephen Lawrence case illustrate, there are those who would retreat from an expansive idea of Britishness into a constricted shell of right-wing English nationalism. My vision of Britain comes not from uniformity but from celebrating diversity, in other words a multi-ethnic and multinational Britain... I understand Britishness as being outward-looking, open, internationalist with a commitment to democracy and to tolerance.

Gordon Brown [1]

The central theme of this report is the role played by government in influencing public attitudes towards ethnic communities and multicultural Britain and how the vision powerfully described above by the Chancellor, Gordon Brown, can be achieved. Over the years political leaders have failed to portray a positive picture of multiculturalism, contributing to the dominant perception of minorities as a 'problem' and fostering a damaging association between immigration policy and internal race relations. The report argues, moreover, that the public's anxiety about multiculturalism is central to its confusion over Britain's changing national identity. New Labour has taken up the challenge to foster a new national identity for the 21st Century and to create a cohesive, inclusive country. If it is to be successful in that task, it needs to address public attitudes towards Britain as a multicultural society, shed some unhelpful assumptions of the past, explore good practice in other western countries and develop a proactive new strategy.

The report demonstrates that the Government has begun to recognise that race is a key issue which can no longer be neglected. Certain significant steps which it has taken, like the establishment of the Stephen Lawrence inquiry, and the tone of its statements on race issues, indicate that it has identified that a new approach is needed. These isolated initiatives, admirable as they are, will be inadequate. What is required is a deliberate cross-departmental strategy to shift the terms of the debate on race and immigration which, if implemented over a long period of time, can achieve the desired objectives of positively influencing public perceptions of multi-culturalism.

The challenge facing political leaders is, on the surface, quite different from that which they faced thirty years ago. But the way in which they responded to this issue has left a historical legacy which they now must address. In 1964, the Conservative candidate for Smethwick was elected on the basis of this racist slogan: 'If you want a nigger neighbour, vote Labour.' This, as Stuart Hall noted was 'the first moment when racism [was] appropriated into the official policy and programme of a major political party and legitimated as the basis of an electoral appeal.'[2] Such tactics would be unthinkable today in mainstream politics, but the spirit of that occasion has haunted politics ever since.

The majority of British politicians now refrain from crude racism. But there are those who still prefer to placate rather than to tackle prejudiced attitudes; attitudes which are now much more likely to be manifested in subtle forms or linked to the still volatile subject of immigration or so called 'bogus' asylum seekers.

Sanctions on behaviour

Government strategy since the 1960s has been to use the law to tackle discriminatory behaviour. The Race Relations Acts and related measures have made a significant contribution to that task and could do more, were the 1976 Act strengthened in ways that the Commission for Racial Equality (CRE) and others have advocated. That Act is indeed now the subject of government review.

The creation of a cohesive society, and mutual respect between diverse Britons, however requires more than legislative sanctions. Understanding may grow out of changed behaviour but this cannot be assumed. The British army recognised this when, in October 1997, it took up the task of eradicating racism from the forces. Its spokesperson expressed the view (on BBC Radio 4) that changes in behaviour alone were insufficient: what was needed was strong leadership within the army to change underlying prejudices and attitudes.

Former Shadow Home Secretary, Roy Hattersley, has observed that legislative sanctions for unacceptable behaviour must be supported by a direct challenge to the attitudes which lie behind that behaviour:

attitudes can be changed by legislation backed up by exhortation – as the increasing antagonism to drink-driving proves.[3]

The example of drinking and driving laws is indeed pertinent here. The law is clear and sets down boundaries. But massive public education campaigns have also been launched in order to change public attitudes so that behaviour changes are not simply to do with a fear of getting caught but with an understanding of the issues and an acceptance of the argument.

In July 1997, the chairman of the CRE, Sir Herman Ouseley, compared the amount of public money spent by the previous government to influence public attitudes on drinking and driving with the minimal resources that had been made available to the CRE to promote positive views on race and multiculturalism.[4]

Some business leaders have recognised the need to take leadership on this issue seriously. Robert Ayling, chief executive of British Airways, acknowledges that:

> As a country we have thrived, improved and become more wealthy by taking the best of the immigrant community and utilising their skills. If we can't break down racist barriers between people we won't work successfully as a company.[5]

National identity

Attitudes towards minorities are inextricably tied to something deeper: the sense of nationhood and how ethnic communities fit into that landscape. Black and Asian people have historically been described, discussed and legislated for on the basis that they were a 'problem' for the nation, not an intrinsic part of nor an asset to it. Their presence has been deemed to be temporary and conditional.[6]

The idea has taken root that these unwanted but tolerated citizens are here under sufferance and expected to behave. The fear that the Britain of the future will be 'contaminated' if too many non-whites are allowed in has been a recurrent theme since the Fifties. Then we had race riots in Notting Hill over miscegenation; in the Nineties we have had panic over the potential arrival of highly skilled Hong Kong residents, described by Norman Tebbit as:

great waves of immigration by people who do not share our
culture, our language, our ways of social conduct, in many
cases who owe no allegiance to our country was, and is, a
destabilising factor in society.[7]

That such language already sounds out of tune with the times is a
testimony to the extent that the current government has already begun
to change the tone of the debate. But Labour has itself a long way to go
before it portrays the positive image of a multicultural Britain to which
it aspires.

New Labour

Labour is the party most black and Asian Britons vote for. Since the
1960s, the party has been responsible for introducing all of the
progressive legislation to end discrimination and promote equal rights
for ethnic minority citizens based on respect for diversity. And yet the
key Labour pre and post election publications in 1997 did not reflect
many positive images of a diverse, multicultural country. In *New Labour
because Britain Deserves Better*,[8] a glossy, well-produced publication,
there are 63 illustrations with approximately 300 recognisable faces of
Britons all giving a strong and positive message about themselves. In
that sea of affirmative images, fifteen of the images are those of black
people, some which appear more than once. One is Nelson Mandela,
eleven are children in three school pictures. You also have a black man
on a merry go round, overshadowed by a white mother and her child.
Only two detectable Asians appear, one is a young professional Asian
man and the other a blurred picture of a South Asian woman. One
young woman student, who could be Middle Eastern or mixed race,
also features under the headline: 'Get the Unemployed From Welfare to
Work.' None of the many happy families are of ethnic minority origin.
One sentence on the multicultural nature of Britain appears in the
section on fighting crime. Except for one small corner of a turban in a
crowd scene, there is no image which shows the cultural diversity of this
nation. No saris for example nor any nor dreadlocks are in evidence.
Another pre-election publication, *Realising Britain's Future* is also
dominated mostly by white images. If you look at any major
commercial catalogue or magazine today – a Mothercare catalogue for

example – you get a wholly different impression of Britain as a diverse, multi-ethnic society. Television advertisements too are beginning to reflect this diversity.

The Labour Party post election celebration magazine[9] was similarly full of images of white people. Bill Morris, General Secretary of the Transport and General Workers Union, is seen talking to a black woman and a white MP. One black actor is seen playing the drum with John Prescott. The bulldog used in the election reappears, fondly patted by Peter Mandelson, in spite of the fact that the bulldog image had been attacked by prominent black people when it was first used.[10] The Manifesto and the other publications made clear the party commitment on promoting equality of opportunity and ending racial violence. But ethnic communities in this country would have to make great leaps to imagine themselves into many of the more general goals set out for Labour policy.

In May 1998, Chris Smith, the Secretary of State for Culture, Media and Sport published a book on creativity in Britain. In it he praised the way the erstwhile Australian Prime Minister Paul Keating had used the nation's cultural life to edge the country towards a new identity which was closer to Asia than Europe. Smith wrote: 'Cultural activity can help us with the development of our sense of who and what we are. It can help therefore to set a sense of direction for our society '[11] And yet in his publication, with one exception, black and Asian artists and designers are only briefly mentioned in two sentences. Ten names appear, including people like Salman Rushdie and Ozwald Boateng, but a whole raft of others like Meera Syal, Lenny Henry, Jatinder Verma are left out.[12]

It is not so long ago that party conference speeches by Tony Blair in 1995 and 1996, then Leader of the Opposition, had echoes of a Thatcherite view of British history. In 1996, he spoke with great passion about this country saying: 'consider a thousand years of British history and what it tells us. The first parliament in the world. The industrial revolution ahead of its time. An empire, the largest empire the world has ever known.'[13] Black and Asian Britons were unlikely to feel much enthusiasm for this particular British achievement, a case of political leadership attempting to address the aspirations of one section of the population at the expense of the rest. The welcome contrast to this speech was Blair's stirring address to the 1997 conference. Britain, he said, could not be a beacon to the world when there was so much real evidence of exclusion of ethnic minorities from key professional areas. He was proud to be providing a vision for a post-imperial new Britain.[14]

It is noticeable that advisors to Ministers, and senior Whitehall officials, are almost exclusively white.[15] There is thus little ongoing regular input by black and Asian Britons into speeches and publications promoting the ideas and images of the Government. The Foreign Office has, however set up a panel of people to advise the department on changing its employment profile and the image given of Britain abroad. A number of dynamic, professional ethnic minority individuals have been co-opted on to the team. In May 1998 the Home Secretary set up the Race Forum, an appointed consultative body consisting of experienced and talented black and Asian Britons to exchange views and ideas at the heart of government.

Labour needs to promote a clear vision of the multicultural Britain to which it aspires. It could be argued that the government is not highlighting the plight of ethnic minorities as a separate issue because it is determined to see them as part of the mainstream population: a declaration of one country politics perhaps. But no clear message had been articulated to indicate that this is what is motivating the leadership. As leader of the opposition, Tony Blair speaking in January 1996 about the stakeholder economy to the Singapore business community, said:

> [It would be an economy in which] opportunity is available to all, advancement is through merit and from which no group or class is set apart or excluded. This is the economic justification for social cohesion, for a fair and strong society.[16]

The problem is that ethnic communities would not assume that they are part of that vision because their inclusion is implicit rather than explicit. If it is the intended message, it should be said out loud. New Labour needs no lessons on how to generate the right images, so why is it neglecting this key area? For too long ethnic minorities have been thought of as outside the mainstream by the political elite and as a consequence by the communities themselves.

One outstanding contribution made by the Labour government within its first year of office was its approach to the Stephen Lawrence murder, a crime motivated by racism which has become a potent symbol of racism in Britain today. Until Labour came to power the political establishment had done little. In 1997 the new Labour Home Secretary set up a public enquiry into the police investigations into that murder and a Home Office Minister has been seen at key memorial events with the Lawrence family. This has, however as yet only happened in this one high profile case.

Mike O'Brien, the Immigration Minister, made a passionate speech at a major conference in the Midlands in November 1997 affirming that the fact that Britain is now a multicultural nation should be a source of pride to all the people of the nation. He included himself and his own family background in his narrative, thus making clear his perception that multiculturalism is an inclusive term, encompassing all Britons, not only minorities.[17] But contrasting speeches and statements on members of minorities seeking to enter from abroad have conveyed a conflicting message. Moreover, isolated speeches from the Minister responsible for race relations are, in themselves, inadequate to challenge entrenched attitudes.

Coherent strategy

The political leadership in Britain needs now to produce a national strategy which takes this issue up with clarity and commitment because it is essential for a mature democracy with a mixed and changing population. It is time for politicians to tackle the widespread resentment, hostility and suspicion between white Britons and the other communities who make up this nation. Although some care is now taken to avoid inflammatory statements, people with political influence need to go further to generate more positive public attitudes towards multiculturalism and to discuss new definitions of what it means to be British. Philip Dodd, in his essay *The Battle Over Britain:*

> So this is the crisis: the need to imagine a usable national identity for the next century. But there is also a further crisis: the failure of leading political and cultural elites to contribute to such an imagining. They are part of the problem.[18]

As the millennium approaches, the aspirations of the nation need to be higher than those which simply aim to contain extreme manifestations of disaffection or which aim for minimal levels of racial tolerance. The children of immigrants want more than equal opportunities. They want respect, recognition and their birthright to be involved citizens of their country. Bhikhu Parekh:

> Respect and recognition are complex concepts. They require that ethnic minorities should be accepted as fellow subjects fully qualified to speak for themselves and to participate in all decisions affecting their lives, including the norms by which they are to be judged. Respect and recognition go beyond equal opportunity and call for a profound change in white society's attitude to ethnic minorities.[19]

Across the European Union and in Britain itself, there is some agreement that public attitudes need to be addressed directly: to ensure that people comply with the law even when they do not fear the sanction of the courts, and to prevent actions which are not illegal but which would have a damaging effect. The day to day lives of people from diverse backgrounds, how they relate in the workplace, neighbourhoods, schools and in personal relations depend on trust and ease which in turn are determined by perceptions and attitudes.

European institutions: focus on public opinion

In the past decade, both the European Parliament and the European Commission have put considerable emphasis on the need to influence public opinion about the position of ethnic minorities within the European Union. Central and local government have, it is felt, largely failed to exercise leadership to foster more positive attitudes.[20] Moreover, political leaders in some countries have proved unwilling to condemn xenophobia and official opposition to racism has been undermined by negative remarks by national politicians. Some have sought to gain popularity by colluding with xenophobic tendencies, leading a representative of the Commission to tell the European Parliament in 1992 that there was concern about the 'deliberate stirring up of xenophobia for political gain':

it is considered necessary that the Governments and
Parliaments of the Member states should act clearly and
unambiguously to counter the sentiments and manifestations
of racism. [21]

The media has also evoked criticism for providing:

information about the minorities ... which is quite often
biased, dwelling at length on the misdemeanours of some
members of the minority groups, giving poor coverage to the
problems of such communities and ignoring almost all of their
achievement.[22]

As long ago as 1988 the Commission argued that legal mechanisms
would not be enough to tackle the root of the problem of prejudice:
'information and communication structures should be reinforced since
xenophobia and racist attitudes are fed by ignorance of others'.[23]

There is also a recognition that fears about immigration and asylum
were creating intense and damaging hostility. A communication from
the European Commission in 1994 on immigration and asylum policies
acknowledged that those issues:

give rise to public and parliamentary debate of growing
intensity and occasionally acts of violence totally out of
character with Europe's traditions and laws ...[W]estern Europe
has a well-established and solidly anchored tradition of respect
for human values and social justice. At the same time there has
been something of a polarisation in the attitudes of different
sectors of society towards the issue of new immigration and
towards established immigrant communities.[24]

The communication argued that there was a lack of knowledge or
acceptance that immigration had been a positive process which had
brought economic and broader cultural benefits both to the host
countries and to the immigrants themselves:

there are ... people who are genuinely concerned by the
perception that large numbers of people are immigrating to

Europe. This, however, is often based on feeling rather than facts. But equally, it is perhaps this perception which has played its part in the increase in the number and ferocity of racially motivated attacks which have scarred the immediate past.

This poses an increasing problem for governments. They must retain credibility with moderate people on both sides of the argument in a situation where the anti-democratic elements have sought to exploit the immigration issue. To counter the dangers this poses, governments need to build on the public's tradition of fairness, by putting more energetic emphasis on the benefits of immigration, both economic and social, while at the same time showing that immigration is under control by putting a coherent long-term strategy in place.

An essential element of this strategy would be to ensure that the public is well informed: public perceptions could be influenced by providing reliable information on actual and potential migratory flows. A good information policy is therefore indispensable. [25]

IPPR research

In order to produce a government strategy to affect public attitudes towards ethnic communities in the UK, it is important to know what these attitudes are and how they have changed since the 1950s when substantial numbers of immigrants first began to arrive from the ex-colonies. What were attitudes then? What are they now? And is it possible to trace changes? This is problematic because surveys into public attitudes towards minorities have been intermittent and, with some exceptions, inadequate since the major piece of research carried out in 1966 for *Colour and Citizenship, A Report on Britain's Race Relations.*[26] Thirty years on there has been nothing to match the scale or depth of that survey.

In order to obtain quantitative and qualitative data on white attitudes towards different minority communities, and inter-ethnic attitudes, with a level of detail not available elsewhere, IPPR commissioned two surveys in 1997. A quantitative survey was carried out by NOP in October 1997 to find out to what extent negative (and positive) attitudes are held by white people of different ages and class background towards Asians, Afro-Caribbeans and Jewish people. It also explored the attitudes of members of those communities towards white people and towards members of the other communities. Following this, in December, a qualitative study was carried out by Opinion Leader Research to explore the reasons which lie behind those attitudes. The results of those surveys, which confirmed the extent to which inter-ethnic attitudes are an obstacle to the creation of a cohesive society, are set out in chapter 2.

Aware that some governments abroad have already developed deliberate strategies to address public opinion, study visits were organised to three countries. Canada was an obvious choice because successive governments have developed strategies and programmes intended to test and influence public attitudes towards visible minority communities and have also drawn on public attitudes when developing their national policies. This interactive, integrated approach is still relatively rare. The author visited Canada in December 1995 and interviewed forty-five people working in various government departments in Ottawa and Toronto and within a number of ethnic community group representatives in Toronto.

The Netherlands was selected because, unlike most other countries in the European Union, the Dutch government has started to tackle the issue of public opinion and perceptions of multiculturalism and in a way that is proactive and innovative. The Dutch government is increasingly concerned about the need to create a more cohesive society and is engaged in developing ideas to enable the population to understand why racism is unacceptable and to feel comfortable with diversity. The study visit was carried out in May 1996. Utrecht, The Hague and Amsterdam were visited and interviews took place with government officials and non-governmental organisations working in the race field.

The final study visit was to the city of Berlin in May/June 1996. In addition to local government officials, interviews were carried out with representatives of ethnic communities and a number of journalists. Berlin has had to manage and accommodate the reintegration of East Berliners. It is also a multiracial city preparing to become the new German capital. Neo-Nazism in Germany is a growing problem and this has a particular resonance for all Europeans. All of these factors have created pressures and opportunities in the country and public institutions in Berlin are spearheading initiatives to educate and influence the attitudes of a local population trying to cope with these major developments.

Interviews were also carried out with individuals, community and institutional representatives, academics, MPs, local authority members and officials in Britain. These interviews helped to establish the nature and the importance of public attitudes towards multiculturalism and also influenced our recommended strategy for government action.

The future

The challenge for the future is for white people to transform their notion of nationhood so that ethnic minority Britons have a place within it. It is also to get black and Asian Britons to see themselves as an integral part of the nation and not at the fringes of it. This cannot happen unless old dilemmas are addressed. How does a government assuage the fear of immigration in British society whilst at the same time valuing the contribution made by immigrants and their descendants? How does the political leadership give messages of inclusion to ethnic communities while still playing the anti-immigration card in order to win or retain popular white support? How does a country, finally coming to terms with a post-imperial past, avoid the temptation to escape to that idealised past? How can you promote better race relations without better discrimination laws, and how can you do the latter if it raises such resentment that you cannot achieve the former? How does a country learn from history without being imprisoned by it? How can the political leadership be persuaded that influencing public attitudes entails following not what the public has been induced into believing, but the exact opposite?

It can be done. We have learnt to change our attitudes radically towards the environment, smoking, drinking, health and child care. There is no reason to assume that racial attitudes cannot be similarly transformed. This report will argue that, as Britain goes into the next century, a more visionary and robust political leadership across the political parties should take up that challenge. Unless we break from some of the negative attitudes of the past, it will not be possible to bring Britain's ethnic communities into the heart of Britain and modernise our perception of Britain's national identity.

Chapter 2 describes the problem as we see it. It reminds us of the facts about multicultural Britain, the success stories as well as the clear evidence of a lack of social cohesion. It sets out what is known about the attitudes which lie behind such social discord and exclusion, including IPPR's own quantitative and qualitative surveys. From that evidence, it defines the challenge which today's political leaders must meet, if they are to redress the prejudice and misunderstandings which divide us.

Chapter 3 explains how we came to be in this position, the historical legacy of failed leadership, equivocation and contradictory messages which allowed negative perceptions to be fostered. Public debate on immigrants and asylum seekers is seen to have played a crucial role in influencing public attitudes to minorities and the non-inclusive perception of multiculturalism which we have inherited.

Chapter 4 advocates a new strategy, drawing on overseas experience of government initiatives to shift attitudes on race, and on successful campaigns here to change public opinion on unrelated issues. It looks at the goal, the message and how, in practical terms, it could be delivered.

2. The challenge

A good society, as John Kenneth Galbraith said in 1994, must be at peace with itself.[27] This chapter shows how from being at peace with itself, this country is, at present, unsettled, looking for an identity and a narrative which makes sense.[28] As we move to the end of this century and enter the next one, Britain is experiencing a post imperial, post-war national identity crisis which has been intensified by the processes of European integration and devolution.[29] Globalisation, too, has contributed to anxieties about national identity, patriotism and loyalty. In spite of the euphoric mood that followed the 1997 election, this country manifestly lacks a positive sense of itself. As Kenan Malik observed in his book *The Meaning of Race:*

> There is in society a lack of vision, an absence of purpose, a failure of will... The ideologies that bound together or gave a sense of purpose to society have collapsed or lost their credibility. The old bonds that held society together are dissolving. New ones have to be forged.[30]

Either political leaders can seize the opportunity to create a new identity which is able to value diversity and internationalism or they can miss this chance and simply encourage people to retreat into a smaller and more exclusive sense of who they are and which community they belong to. The national debate over Europe is partly about these choices. The management of a country adapting to these great changes requires great skill and imagination.

Meeting this challenge is a project that the New Labour government has taken up with some enthusiasm and it could be argued that the country voted overwhelmingly for Labour in 1997 because that was one of its declared intentions. Tony Blair, in *The Spectator* Lecture in 1995, said:

> Individuals prosper best within a strong and cohesive society... A society which is fragmented and divided, where people feel no sense of shared purpose, is unlikely to produce well-adjusted and responsible citizens [31]

Labour's adaptation of communitarian politics illustrates the search for new models of citizenship and solidarity. There is a quest for a new joint sense of purpose, a seeking for a balance between a culture of rights and responsibilities, a society where personal achievement goes hand in hand with a wider sense of belonging.

If Britain is not as harmonious and cohesive as the Government believes it should be, several factors have contributed to this state of affairs. Racial disharmony is crucial amongst them. Without dealing with this area of social dissonance even the most inspired aspirations for society are unlikely to be realised.

Multiculturalism and multiracialism, unless integrated into this sweeping agenda, could threaten, and be threatened by, all of this rethinking. Communitarian politics, if promoted, must be inclusive of all communities. As Anna Coote has warned:

> Communities like clubs are defined as much by exclusion as inclusion. Where does communitarianism leave the dissenters, the non-conformists, the artist and the innovators, the misfits and the migrants...?[32]

And the fissures which are manifesting themselves across the country are not only between white and non-white Britons. Some young Muslims, Hindus, Sikhs and black people, are choosing to opt out of even the most basic kind of integration.[33] Tensions in areas like Southall, which were once strong multiracial communities are manifestly signs of disintegration.[34]

The ideal to promote is that of an inter-dependent, organic community which is able to sustain diversity. This means enabling people within diverse communities to live together with mutual respect, some key shared values and an understanding that they cannot survive as racially or culturally segregated units in the modern world. This cannot be achieved unless racial and religious tensions and differences are dealt with.

Multicultural Britain

The question to ask is why British society is still racially divided and troubled about multiculturalism fifty years after large scale immigration began. There has been some progress, but less than might have been expected and less too than is frequently assumed.[35] Perhaps more importantly, progress has been *uneven*. While there are clear indicators of social exclusion, of discrimination, harassment and inequality, black and Asian Britons have more opportunities than ever before, and in many areas are making a positive impact on British life which is out of all proportion to their numbers.[36] Signs of de facto integration are visible in all walks of life. But the subjective understanding of these developments, how they are seen and evaluated by many white Britons, presents a more pessimistic picture. This gap in perception needs to be addressed.

Black and Asian Britons form only a small proportion of the total national population but as most of them live within our conurbations, urban Britain is now, in its composition, indisputably and irreversibly multicultural. Just over 3 million people from ethnic minorities live in the UK. Two thirds of Caribbeans, a third of Chinese residents and the majority of children in every ethnic community are British born. Intermarriage between white Britons and black and Asian Britons continues to rise. Among those born in Britain, half of Caribbean men, a third of Caribbean women and a fifth of Asian men have a white partner.[37] An NOP survey carried out in 1996 revealed that 40% of young black people consider themselves British rather than Africans or Afro-Caribbeans.[38]

The transformation of most large British cities have into cosmopolitan places gives cause for considerable optimism. Tensions do exist and periodically there have been moments of serious unrest, but such problems are less widespread and intractable than they are in the USA. The issue of the 'colour line', which William De Bois saw as the biggest problem of the twentieth century, has not emerged in this country in quite the stark way that one sees in American cities. There has not been a massive white flight into the suburbs. A white person can still walk in Southall or Brixton in London or St Paul's in Bristol and not feel that it is demarcated territory where his or her presence is seen as unacceptable; correspondingly, black and Asian people can now be found in the most affluent of white areas.[39] The difference is also clear when one compares Britain with European countries. In France, for example, although mixed communities live in close proximity in some of the most deprived urban areas, it is rare to see middle class neighbourhoods which have any significant ethnic minority presence.[40]

Considerable economic and educational progress has been achieved by some. Black and Asian Britons are much more likely than white Britons to continue their education post-16 and, with the exception of Caribbean men and Bangladeshi women, people from ethnic communities are more likely to go to university than their white peers. Indian, African, Asian and Chinese children are doing better educationally than the white population.[41] Eighty three per cent of Indians living in Britain are owner occupiers. The Commission for Racial Equality publication, *Roots For the Future* is an impressive record of ethnic minority achievements. Many of Britain's self-made millionaires are from the ethnic communities and 23 per cent of doctors in the National Health Service were born abroad.[42] In his introduction to *Roots of the Future*, Prince Charles comments on the role played by members of ethnic communities in changing life in Britain:

> [Their] contribution is incredibly wide and varied – from the economy, politics, public service and the law, medicine, the arts and even our cooking. It is a contribution which today forms part of our national identity, and it adds immeasurably to the richness and creativity of modern Britain.[43]

Exclusion

Inequality and exclusion, however, persist at every level. When it comes to positions of influence and power, black and Asian Britons are seriously under-represented. Out of 651 MPs, only 6 are from the minorities. There are no High Court judges or national newspaper editors, and there is only one high ranking police officer and fewer than five civil servants above Grade 5.[44] Speaking in 1997, the Prime Minister said:

> We cannot be a beacon to all the world unless the talents of all the people shine through. Not one black high court judge; not one chief black constable or permanent secretary; not one black army officer above the rank of colonel. Not one Asian either.[45]

Two recent reports by the MP Keith Vaz have revealed that Asians in particular are seriously underrepresented in new public appointments and in the civil service hierarchy.[46]

Direct racial discrimination continues to be experienced by a significant section of the black and Asian population. In particular, Bangladeshis, Pakistanis and young Caribbean men are the most likely to face discrimination and, in part as a result, poverty is also a serious problem in these groups. A report by Richard Berthoud in 1998 confirmed that these two are now the poorest groups in Britain and that the rate of poverty in the two communities is four times that for the white community.[47] Unemployment among young black men in London is over 60 per cent and the ethnic minorities suffer disproportionately in times of recession.[48] Many young people in these communities have started to disengage from the political process because of these experiences. In the 1997 election, a pre-election MORI poll found that among Afro-Caribbeans aged under 25, only 16 per cent intended to vote.[49] Pakistanis, Bangladeshis, sections of the Indian population and Afro-Caribbeans still suffer serious disadvantages in British society. More than 80 per cent of Pakistanis and Bangladeshis live in households whose income is below half the national average. There is increasing evidence of 'cultural racism' directed against the Muslim community in particular.[50] Twenty years after the last Race Relations Act came into force, racism, discrimination and structural inequality remain facts of life for black and Asian Britons of all ages.

Harassment

If white people face difficult economic and social conditions, scapegoating the outsider is likely to get worse. The Association of London Authorities, in its submission to the House of Commons Home Affairs Committee, described these social factors and their impact:

> ... key factors in the shaping of racist attitudes [include] employment, competition for adequate housing, a lack of leisure facilities for young people etc... People find scapegoats to blame for their situation and focus on visible newcomers at the same time as seeing their scapegoating legitimised by the state.[51]

In 1991, the British Crime Survey estimated that there were over 130,000 racially motivated incidents in Britain between 1990 and

1991.[52] Other studies indicate that the majority of the perpetrators are young and white with deeply held hostile attitudes towards minority groups.[53]

The most recent PSI survey shows that 250,000 Caribbeans and Asians experience racial harassment every year.[54] A report on racial harassment and violence by the All-Party Parliamentary Group on Race and Community concluded:

> It would hardly be an exaggeration to say that one in every two Afro-Caribbean and Asian families suffered directly or indirectly from the effects of racial incidents in 1991.[55]

The harassment occurs within a context of hostile attitudes where such behaviour is not regarded as deviant. A 1997 Home Office report, *The Perpetrators of Racial Harassment and Racial Violence* concluded:

> Based on existing evidence and evidence from two case study areas [the report] paints a picture which suggests that the perpetrators of the most violent racist assaults do not act in a social vacuum. They carry out their assaults in areas in which all age groups across the local community share common attitudes to ethnic minorities, where people of all ages, including very young children and older adults, regularly engage in the verbal abuse and intimidation of ethnic minorities.[56]

In the All Party report, Peter Lloyd, then Minister of State in the Home Office, accepted that even relatively minor incidents can be:

> cumulatively hugely important for those who suffer them personally, very distressing over a period of time, and very corrosive in the sense of creating distress and fear.[57]

Racism in the shires and rural areas has been growing and new-Fascist groups have turned their attention to those areas for recruitment and financial support.[58] There is also concern over the manifestation of conflicts between ethnic and religious groups.[59]

Islamaphobia

Signs of increasingly virulent anti-Muslim attitudes are manifest across Europe. With the end of the Cold War, Islam is increasingly portrayed as the new enemy of the West by the media, by some politicians, especially in the European Parliament and by academics.[60] Twenty years ago, although there was some suspicion of Arab nations and people, westerners did not display the levels of anti-Islamic prejudices found today. This reveals all too clearly how racism and xenophobia do not remain constant and consistent. They mutate, find new ways of expression and new targets for hatred.

The Runnymede Trust which established a Commission to look into this new and fast growing area of concern, stated in its interim consultation document in 1997:

> Islamaphobia ... has existed in western countries and cultures for several centuries but in the last twenty years has become more explicit, more extreme and dangerous. [61]

A MORI poll in December 1990 showed that 85 per cent of those questioned felt that they knew little or nothing about Islam and a quarter thought that Muslims were intolerant, fanatical or extremist.

There is evidence of opinion makers across the political spectrum effectively seeking to establish Islam as the new post-Communist threat to the free world. The American political scientist Professor Samuel Huntingdon, in an influential article, The Clash of Civilisations, argued that an irreconcilable gulf of ideas separated Islam from the fundamental values of the west. Islam, he sees as fanatic and irrational, the west as its opposite.[62]

The editor of *The Daily Telegraph* Charles Moore wrote in *The Spectator*:

> We want foreigners as long as their foreignness is not overwhelming... Britain is basically English speaking, and Christian, and if one starts to think it might become Urdu speaking and Muslim and brown, one gets angry and frustrated. [63]

Conor Cruise O'Brien denounced Islam as a 'repulsive religion'[64] in *The Times* and it was in the same newspaper that Bernard Levin, wrongly assuming that the Oklahoma bomb was the work of Muslims, thundered that soon the town would be called 'Khartoum on the Mississippi'.[65]

Respected journalist Clare Hollingworth wrote in the *International Herald Tribune* in 1993:

> Muslim fundamentalism is fast becoming the chief threat to global peace and security as well as a cause of national and local disturbance through terrorism. It is akin to the menace posed by Nazism and Fascism in the 1930s and then by Communism in the 50s.[66]

There are counter-voices emerging in this new and dangerous confrontation. People like the MEP Glynn Ford and Professor Tariq Modood and many others reject such views believing talk of clashes to be irresponsible and dangerous. They make connections between this kind of rhetoric and the attitudes displayed by white Europeans towards the mostly law abiding Muslims in their midst.

Professor Fred Halliday believes not only that anti-Islamic feelings are rising in Europe, but that these feelings tap into ancient sources of enmity making them potentially lethal:

> For some, particularly those who advocate it, hostility to Muslims requires no justification since it is itself a legitimate response to the threats, and the militant rhetoric that emerge from the Muslim world itself.'[67]

Anti-Semitism

Anti-Semitism has always been much more of a threat in mainland Europe than in Britain, not least because extreme right wing parties like the National Front have a real presence in mainstream politics. But this does not mean that the problem does not exist in this country. The Runnymede Trust report *A Very Light Sleeper*:

> Anti-Semitism, is deeply embedded in European societies and ... is present in all countries... Anti-Semitic incidents –

cemetery desecrations, arson attacks, physical damage of property, the daubing of anti-Semitic graffiti – occur regularly, but there have been few direct physical attacks on persons. Such incidents often have a greater impact, by instilling fear and uncertainty into small Jewish communities.[68]

In the foreword of the report, Lord Lester of Herne Hill wrote:

This report demonstrates that anti-Semitism is alive and – literally – kicking in Britain today... Violent racial prejudice and hostility are not confined to non-white minorities, nor is anti-Semitism itself a purely European phenomenon.[69]

Between 1993 and 1996 there has been some anecdotal evidence of anti-Semitism in Britain. Jewish graves have been desecrated in Edinburgh[70] and Southampton.[71] A synagogue was violated in North London, and a Jewish investment banker described the overt anti-Jewish feelings openly expressed in the City.[72] Appalling anti-Semitism, as experienced by one Jewish family in middle class Twickenham, was described in the *Mail on Sunday*[73] and a survey found that 12 per cent of white Britons said that they would not like to live next to a Jew. 25 per cent of people interviewed believed that the problem was likely to get worse over the next few years.[74]

Action against discrimination

Twenty years ago Roy Jenkins, then Home Secretary, made a momentous speech to the National Council for Commonwealth Immigrants. In it he outlined his passionate belief that integration was essential if we were to avoid the race problems which were erupting in the United States. He said integration should not mean:

the loss, by immigrants, of their own national characteristics and culture. I do not think we need in this country a 'melting pot'... It would deprive us of most of the positive benefits of immigration which I believe to be very great indeed. I define integration, therefore, not as a flattening process of assimilation, but as equal opportunity, accompanied by cultural diversity in an atmosphere of mutual tolerance. [75]

These enlightened aspirations remain only partially fulfilled. The Race Relations Acts and related equal opportunities policies, implemented over the following decades, have reduced the incidence of overt discrimination. They have had a significant impact on employers, public and private, and on public discourse. Overt racism has been made sufficiently unacceptable that even those who do have strongly held negative views of black and Asian people, tend to prefix their opinions with disclaimers. The kind of race discrimination we now have in this country is often subtle and disguised or indirect.

There are those who believe that the laws have had a more profound effect on British life. Jack Straw speaking on the twentieth anniversary of the 1976 Race Relations Act:

> Today we are witnessing the fruits of the race relations legislation introduced by Labour governments. This has undeniably advanced the cause of racial integration in British society. Not only has it changed the legal framework to prevent discrimination on grounds of race and colour, *it has also succeeded in changing attitudes.*[76] (my emphasis)

It is indisputable that attitudes have shifted but the surveys conducted for IPPR for this project, set out below, present a complex picture of these changes. Although the nature of racism has changed and the most blatant manifestations of prejudice have become socially unacceptable, public perceptions have not yet progressed to the point where there is an overwhelming endorsement of multiracial, multiethnic Britain. Existing measures have failed to establish the kind of positive attitudes between white people and members of minority communities which are necessary for a cohesive, inclusive, multi-cultural society.

Survey evidence of public opinion

Research into social attitudes is carried out regularly in Britain. What is less common is regular, substantive research into attitudes towards race and multiculturalism. In the United States[77] and Canada detailed and varied research on racial attitudes is routinely undertaken by academics and by government departments. In the United States there is now a substantial body of research into the changing identities of white Americans and into what influences their attitudes towards ethnic minorities.

For at least two decades the emphasis in the UK has been on studying racial discrimination, racial disadvantage and racial violence; on behaviour rather than attitudes. There has been little interest in the role of prejudice in discriminatory behaviour and the persistence (or not) of prejudiced attitudes towards non-white Britons. There has also been some hostility to this kind of work.[78]

Three of the major PEP and Policy Studies Institute surveys into discrimination have included questions on attitudes as have some of the *British Social Attitudes* surveys. There have also been a few media-led surveys such as that commissioned by *The Daily Express* in 1995.[79] In the past decade the European Commission has itself commissioned EU wide attitude surveys which have provided some evidence on how the residents of the member states have responded to the arrival of immigrants and how they perceive their racially and ethnically changed societies. In the absence of substantial domestic information, these are useful indicators of what is happening across Europe, although the differences between countries make it difficult to reach anything other than very generalised conclusions. Relevant findings of some of these surveys are summarised below.

Most studies based their findings on quantitative research. Detailed national *qualitative* research on racial attitudes had not been done until the IPPR commissioned its survey for this report. Inter-ethnic attitudes, also part of the IPPR research, have not hitherto been studied, possibly because the subject has been felt to be too sensitive and because of concern that such information would be used by those who prefer to excuse white racial hostility as something that is part of human nature.[80] Some useful qualitative research with particular groups has been carried out[81] but these have been local to certain geographical areas or group specific. Useful deductions can be made from these but a degree of caution is needed.

There are also inherent difficulties in measuring attitudes and it is right to be cautious about the results. Asking people if they are prejudiced is unlikely to provide answers that are always accurate and honest. People who are prejudiced often do not realise that they are or do not wish to admit to negative attitudes. Feelings can be affected by events and change temporarily. As awareness of racism has grown, declarations of prejudices have become increasingly socially unacceptable. In the 1967 PEP report on race discrimination in Britain, WW Daniel wrote:

> Most of the informants had certain inhibitions that made it difficult for them to be fully explicit about their attitudes and policies towards coloured immigrants.[82]

To overcome this reserve, questions on prejudice for quantitative surveys are often designed to encourage people to talk about others rather than themselves. This model, developed by, among others, the authors of the *British Social Attitudes Surveys*, is now generally accepted as a fairly reliable way of gauging attitudes. The conclusions one can draw out of the answers are not testable in the way that discriminatory behaviour can be measured. But whatever the complexities and limitations of carrying out this research, there can be little doubt that information is important for policy makers concerned about race relations.

Surveys commissioned by the media

An ICM poll for *The Guardian* in 1995[83], with a sample size over 1000, showed awareness of racial prejudice and discrimination among white Britons with only a tiny minority, 3 per cent, describing themselves as very prejudiced:

- 79 per cent of white Britons thought that there was widespread racial prejudice against black people.

- Prejudice did not seem significantly affected by class.

- Those who were prejudiced were more likely to be Conservative voters, to be men and over the age of 65.

An ICM poll for *The Daily Express* in 1995[84], with a sample group of 1,042, found what was possibly some of the most disturbing evidence that has appeared in recent years:

- Two thirds of white people admitted to being at least a little racist.

- There was majority support for repatriation of ethnic minorities.

- 26 per cent said they would, or might, vote for a Le Pen type party.

- Nearly a third of people between the ages of 18-44 said that they would not be happy if someone from an ethnic community moved in next door.

Yet in the same survey some positive attitudes were revealed:

- 63 per cent said that ethnic minorities made a healthy contribution to society.

- 72 per cent said that the black and Asian MPs did a good job.

- Younger people felt more at ease with multiculturalism.

This survey suggests that contradictory feelings exist in the white British population about race, difference and multiculturalism. The fact that prejudice was still so strong was a surprise for many of the politicians commenting on this study.[85]

A BBC study in 1996 showed that one third of the white British population believed racism to be a greater problem than five years previously. The same study found that 61 per cent of white people thought Asians were victims of prejudice and that six out of ten black people in Britain had suffered physical or verbal abuse.[86]

An MTV survey of young people's attitudes in Europe, published in February 1997 showed British youngsters to be the most intolerant in Europe with 30 per cent disagreeing that all races are equal; in Germany the figure was 19 per cent. 30 per cent of British youngsters admitted to having committed at least one racist act; 26 per cent said they would not marry out and less than half were in favour of immigration, even though 55 per cent accepted that multiculturalism had enhanced the country.[87]

British Social Attitudes Surveys[88] 1983-96

These surveys are perhaps the best indicators of change over time because attitudes to race and immigration have been studied periodically since 1983 using the same or similar questions.

Key findings in 1996/97 included the following:

- The support for anti-discrimination legislation is high – between two-thirds and three quarters of the population.

- There had been a sharp drop in the proportion of people who would object to having an ethnic minority boss.

- With regard to the views of whites on the acceptability of other white people marrying Asians or blacks, there was little change between 1983 and 1996. When it came to an assessment of inter-marriage within their own families, the acceptability rates were much higher than before.

There were, however, also less positive findings:

- There was support for hard line immigration policies, and in particular for control of non-white immigration. Asked if they were in favour of less settlement by particular groups, the response for Australians was 30 per cent and for people from the European Union was 40 per cent. But 60 per cent favoured less settlement from the Indian subcontinent and 54 per cent from the West Indies.

- 1n 1983, 54 per cent of people believed that there was prejudice against Asians. In 1996, the figure had risen to 60 per cent. The figure for black people had, however, dropped from 51 per cent to 49 per cent which confirms the view of the authors of the fourth PSI study (below) that those perceived to be *culturally* different are suffering increasing prejudice.

- 40 per cent believed that racism was likely to get worse in the next few years.

The 1996 survey revealed:

> Illiberalism is evident in our views of foreigners. Significant evidence of xenophobia is uncovered with nearly two thirds of English people saying the number of immigrants should be cut and a quarter saying immigrants increase crime.[89]

Ethnic Minorities in Britain, Policy Studies Institute (1997)[90]

In 1994 PSI interviewed a national sample of 2,867 white adults:

- 52 per cent agreed that Asian and black people 'are making a positive contribution to various aspects of British society'. 19 per cent disagreed.

- 25 per cent said that they would describe themselves as prejudiced against Asians (4 per cent 'very' and 21 per cent 'a little'). 20 per cent said that they were prejudiced against Caribbeans (3 per cent 'very' and 17 per cent 'a little'), and 9 per cent against Chinese people.

- 24 per cent said that they would mind if a close relative married a person of ethnic minority origin (14 per cent 'very much' and 10 per cent 'a little'). When asked about the views of others, 52 per cent said they thought that most white people would mind.

- 27 per cent said that they would prefer their children's school to have less than one tenth of its pupils from minority groups. By contrast, 46 per cent said that the ethnic mix of the school would have no influence on their choice, and a further 8 per cent said that it was 'not very important'. There was a strong age effect: among over-50s, 39 per cent said that they would prefer a school with less than one tenth minorities, compared with only 15 per cent of 16-34s.

Eurobarometer Studies 1989 and 1996[91]

These Eurobarometer surveys were based on a representative sample of the citizens of the member states and provide some comparative data to that on the UK population. The 1989 survey focused on civil liberties, rights and opinions about 'others'. It also examined opinions on immigration policy in the European Community. Allowances were made by the researchers for the fact that individual countries vary considerably in the numbers of visible minorities, in their immigration trends, and in the groups which have settled and the causes of migration:

The key findings of the 1989 survey were these:

'Otherness'

'Otherness' as defined by nationality, race, religion, culture and social class was explored by the researchers:

- In Denmark, France, the Netherlands and the United Kingdom, respondents associated 'others' with populations which are culturally distinct from European cultures.

- All countries except for France and the United Kingdom identified black people as the 'other' race. In France, however, it tended to be Arabs and in the UK it was mostly applied to Asians.

- In the European Union the 'other' religion was clearly Islam. Islam was mentioned by more than half of the respondents in Belgium and France and by people in Denmark, Germany and the Netherlands. In the United Kingdom at that time, Islam was not particularly prominent. The fieldwork for this study predated the Rushdie affair.

- The majority of Europeans believed that there was considerable diversity in Europe, but one in three people believed that there were too many people of another nationality or race in his/her country.

- There was a correlation between a strong sense of national pride and a feeling that there were 'too many foreigners around.'

- Advancing age, a lower education level, a tendency towards 'materialism' and right wing leanings were associated with the feeling that there were too many 'others'. Those who were more highly educated and in higher income groups, and those with left wing leanings and notions of leadership, public good and less inclined towards materialism were more likely to attach importance to human rights and to opposing racism.

- Not many EC citizens said that they mixed with 'others' in their neighbourhood or considered them their friends although one in three Europeans has occupational contact with 'others'. Contact made little difference to the degree of intolerance.

- A very small minority of people in Europe blamed 'others' for a rise in delinquency or neighbourhood disputes. Only 12 per cent thought that the presence of people from other nationalities and races reduced property values and 16 per cent believed that their children pulled down education standards.

● Only five percent of the EU population saw immigration as the most important problem facing their country.

● Nearly half of the EU population strongly believed that immigrants were a negative factor for the future, but nearly half of the European population saw their presence as a positive factor.

● 8 out of 10 people disapproved of racist movements.

● One in ten Europeans appeared to show sympathy for racist organisations concerned about immigration.

● Even among the most educated, people who defined themselves as left wing, 7 per cent approved of racist movements.

In Great Britain, only 6 per cent felt immigrants were a positive thing for the future. A quarter of Britons felt that too many ethnic minority children pulled down standards of education. The figure for the Netherlands was 41 per cent. The 1989 Barometer survey went on to develop a typology of the attitudes of respondents bringing together their support of democracy, the extent to which they found the presence of others in the country disturbing and their opinions on the rights of minorities:

Type 1: Those who believe in democracy, do not find the presence of others disturbing and wish to extend the rights of immigrants

Italians	49%
Spaniards	34%
Germans	11%
Britons	8%

22% of all those interviewed fell into that category.

Type 2: Those who support democracy and do not find the presence of others a problem, but do not want to extend rights

Danish	42%
Netherlands	41%
British	38%
Germany	38%
Italy	7%

28% of all those interviewed fell into that category.

The findings of these surveys indicate that there are significant differences in attitudes towards settled minorities and immigrants between European countries. In the UK, any strategy for change would have to be appropriate to this country in order to have an effect. Therefore, even if there are commonly agreed actions within the EU, – like the European Year against Racism – the particular activities and projects undertaken will have to be tailor made for each country. In the UK for example, simply concentrating on the extension of rights for ethnic minorities could have a counterproductive effect on public attitudes, unless there is substantial public awareness work to precede such developments.

1997 Eurobarometer survey

For this survey, 16,154 people were interviewed in the fifteen member states.

The complete report is due to be published at the end of 1998, but some interim findings have been released:

- Nearly one third of European citizens describe themselves as very or quite racist.

- 35 per cent of UK interviewees said that they were not at all racist.

- 32 per cent described themselves as very or quite racist.

- Job insecurity was a major factor influencing the prejudice. Fear of unemployment rather than unemployment itself was the key influence.

- The majority of white Europeans agreed that race discrimination existed and that it was wrong.

- Nearly half believed that too many minority children in schools lowered standards.

- A third were of the opinion that ethnic minorities should 'give up their culture' and assimilate.

IPPR Qualitative and Quantitative Surveys

The data we have outlined provides some indicators of public opinion in the UK but was insufficiently detailed for our own study. In 1996, therefore, the IPPR commissioned NOP to carry out a quantitative study on attitudes and Opinion Leader Research to carry out a parallel qualitative study. The latter, it was felt, would allow for a more honest and intricate explorations of a sensitive subject than was possible with quantitative studies. But as studies based on focus groups are not statistically significant, a quantitative study was also necessary. The IPPR studies broke new ground by examining inter-ethnic attitudes and the views of white and black people in positions of influence.

The aim of the surveys was to give a more textured, in depth view of what white attitudes were towards different ethnic communities, towards immigrants and asylum seekers, and towards the Race Relations Act. Because previous research had been patchy, it is not possible to assess whether attitudes have changed over the years. What is clear, however, is that different indicators show that negative attitudes still persist; that new fears have come into being and that the picture is more complex today than it was in 1969.

The IPPR/NOP survey

A survey of 933 white people was conducted over the telephone using Computer Assisted Telephone Interviewing. 282 Asians and 252 Afro-Caribbeans were also interviewed in person at home and 252 Jewish people by telephone. The survey was carried out in October-November 1996. Geographical, gender and class variations were built into the sample selections.

The main survey findings included:

- Only 6 per cent of white respondents said that there was no race prejudice directed at minority groups in this country. 94% believed that there was at least a little prejudice with 46% saying that people were very, or quite, prejudiced.

- Immigration was not a particularly important issue among the general public. The top issues that concerned them were education, unemployment and crime.

- There was widespread support for refugees although one in every two whites were concerned about refugees causing problems for Britain with the figures being particularly high for older people and for Conservative voters. Asians were as likely to be concerned as whites. They were also more likely to be sceptical about genuine refugees.

- The public were concerned about illegal immigration but only one per cent of white people thought that the issue was among the most serious confronting the country.

- Asians and whites thought that there was too much immigration from South Asia and Africa.

- Three in four whites, Afro-Caribbeans and Jews did not believe that prejudice would decline if all immigration was banned but 22 per cent agreed with the suggestion that it would.

- The elderly and those in the lower socio-economic groups were more likely to believe that racial prejudice would decline if all immigration was banned.

- A quarter of white people felt that Asians and Afro-Caribbeans get too much help from the state.

Intermarriage

- 33 per cent of white, 38 per cent of Asians and 49 per cent of Jews think most people in Britain would mind if one of their close relatives was to marry an Afro-Caribbean.

- 74 per cent of whites said that they themselves would not mind, the figure for young people rising to 88 per cent. 77 per cent of those in the higher socio-economic groups said that they would not mind.

- Only 47 per cent of Asians and 46 per cent of Jews would not mind.

- A third of whites felt that most people in Britain would 'mind a lot' if a close relative were to marry an Asian. Afro-Caribbeans and Jews in particular, thought that most white people would mind.

- One in ten whites and Afro-Caribbeans said that they personally would mind if a close relative were to marry an Asian. Jewish people, 27 per cent were more likely than average to mind a lot if a close relative were to marry an Asian. Seven out of ten whites said that they would not mind, with younger people and those from higher socio-economic groups less likely to mind.

- One in eight whites felt that most people in Britain would mind if a close relative were to marry a Jewish person. When asked if they personally would mind, 5 per cent of whites said they would and 30 per cent of Asians agreed.

Targets of prejudice

- Whites perceived the main targets of prejudice to be Pakistanis (44 per cent), Indians (37 per cent) Caribbeans (33 per cent) and Africans (31 per cent).

- Only five per cent of whites were felt to be victims of prejudice.

Reasons given for prejudice

- The most common reason given for prejudice was to do with unemployment. Economic uncertainty is becoming a powerful disincentive to support multiculturalism. 'They take our jobs' was frequently stated. The second most common reason given was cultural difference and a 'failure to assimilate'.

- Comments about housing, benefits, and people 'exploiting the welfare system' also featured.

Positive responses

- Asked about positive attributes of different ethnic minority groups, Afro-Caribbeans were seen as good at sport and music and to have strong family values. Asians were perceived as hard working and intelligent and as having contributed to British food. Jews were seen as law-abiding, hard working, intelligent and positive contributors to the economy.

- Attitudes towards the Race Relations Act were positive in the case of two thirds of whites interviewed. 35 per cent felt that it is too weak and not enforced properly.

- 69 per cent of white people questioned thought that Afro-Caribbeans had strong family values and 60 per cent thought they contributed to public services.

- 90 per cent thought Asians had strong family values, 77 per cent thought they were intelligent and 72 per cent thought they had contributed positively to the economy.

- Only 7 per cent thought that Asians faced prejudice because they 'lived off benefits' and only 15 per cent associated the crime of mugging with Afro-Caribbeans.

Qualitative survey conducted by opinion leader research for the IPPR

This was the first time in Britain that such research had been carried out. The qualitative project, carried out in the Winter of 1996/7, was intended to complement the NOP survey. Such surveys are not intended to provide statistical information but in depth data which can be used to interpret quantitative findings. With race, a difficult subject to discuss, and an issue on which there can be privately held views which are not openly expressed, this kind of research is invaluable.

Ten extended group discussions were held with white Britons of different gender, age and social class in varying locations around England. There were eight people in each group. Two further 'special' groups were part of this study. They were an opinion leaders group and a young people's group, both in London.

Eight paired in depth interviews were also carried out. The interviewees were:

Pakistani women	(50+)
Black men	(18-35)
Jewish women	(35-40)
Bangladeshi men	(18-35)
Kenyan Hindu women	(35-50)
Indian Sikh men	(35-50)

The key findings of the IPPR/OLR qualitative survey are set out below.

White anxieties

Increasingly, white people of all classes are feeling deep anxieties about the loss of white identity as we go into the next century and into further integration with Europe. Many are now identifying themselves as English rather than British because, as one of the interviewees said, 'A Chinese person could be British, but I am English'. White A/B men, usually assumed to be confident in their identity, are beginning to have their doubts. Others in various socio-economic groups are also expressing self doubt and worry.

Comments like this were made:

'I can't think of any British achievements' or 'The great days are gone forever'.

'I'm English. All my family comes from here.'

White woman (C1/C2)

'Increasingly we are English ...Its a feeling of being beleaguered.'

White man (A/B)

Anxieties about the 'other' were expressed in this way:

'They have brought Britain to its knees'

White woman (C1/C2)

'Britain was a world leader before we had ethnic minorities.'

White man (A/B)

For the young, 'Britishness' has little tangible meaning. Participants defined the qualities of 'Britishness' as:

● Law abiding

● Decency

● 'Tolerance of others we feel to be inferior'

The frustration at the loss of identity and pride has found its manifestation in an increasing undercurrent of racist sympathy and intolerance of difference.

There is a positive British identity which is associated with being a 'gentleman', and the qualities listed above. There is also a negative Britishness which is associated with yobbos, racists and aggression.

The internal contradiction between a hatred of personal racism and having racial prejudices, or in believing in the fairness of this country and yet accepting that it is unfair, remain unresolved.

Fear of the 'other' is based on ignorance. Participants expressed the view that difference should not be celebrated but that everyone should become 'British'. Yet mixed marriages were contentious and mixed race children difficult to accept.

Comments included:

'Someone comes over here and tries to run their country inside ours.'

White man (A/B)

'They try to live by their own religious laws. But this is England and we have English laws. Are they not good enough or something'

White man (C1/C2)

'When you mix ethnicity you are asking for trouble.'

White man (A/B)

'There would be problems with mixed race kids – particularly when some in the same family come out white and others don't.'

White man (A/B)

'I feel I would not have a lot in common with ethnic races and they would not have anything in common with me.'

Jewish woman (A/B)

'We have pandered to all these people who have come in; their rights, their cultures, their way of living. Living in this country is a privilege. You have to be English to live in this country'.

White man (A/B)

Economic anxiety

Increased economic insecurity is creating hostility towards ethnic minorities. Asians and Jewish people are most resented because they are stereotyped as hard working and willing to work all hours.

Comments included:

'They take our jobs, our houses, they grab everything. If you are British, you're a second class citizen'

White man (A/B)

'I worry about my job now. We used to be factory fodder, but now it is much harder to get a job.'

White man(C1/C2)

'They get handouts we can't get – the second they get off the plane.'

White man (C1/C2)

Immigration

The decline of the country was, for some, associated with immigration.

'We let anyone in. Enoch Powell was right'

Jewish woman (A/B)

'We should be more picky'

White woman (C1/C2)

'A lot of intolerance stems from the fact that we are being overwhelmed.'

White man (A/B)

Racism on the rise or things are getting better?

People from ethnic minorities believe the former:

'English people just don't like us being here, they think we are not doing anything.'

Pakistani woman (C1/C2)

'We will never be recognised as part of the country even if we work hard.'

Sikh man

Sources of prejudice
Asked about the sources of other peoples negative attitudes towards minorities, the answers included:

The media

'When did you last see on the media a young black man helping an old white lady?'

White woman (A/B)

Personal experience

'I would never do business with Asians. They don't pay up.'

White man (C1/C2)

The family

'Children aren't racist until they start listening to adults. – you're not born a racist.'

White woman (D/E)

PC backlash

There is a perception that this country has become too politically correct.

'You can't even say blackboard now. It is ridiculous.'

White woman (C1/C2)

Four distinct groups of people which emerged from this survey:

i. The 'Die Hards'

Typically would say: 'I hate them. I admit it'.
Their racism is strong and freely expressed. It is rooted in economic fear and this group often feels depressed and powerless about their own situation.

ii. The 'I'm Not Racist But's...'

Typically would say: I don't care what colour someone's skin is but they can't come over here and get more than we do.'

They rationalise their feelings, presenting them as common sense. They do not see themselves as racists. They often have little personal experience of ethnic minorities.

iii. The 'Comfortable Liberals'

Typically would say: 'Having a good education helps you to see how stupid racism is'.

Well educated professionals, they are anti-racist but feel that the wider problem of racism is not easily solved.

iv. The 'Young Optimists'

Typically would say: 'Racists are stupid. How can you judge everything just by the colour they are?'.

This younger group is the most racially integrated with friends and colleagues from different ethnic backgrounds. Their idealism and anti-racism is instinctive.

Inter-ethnic attitudes

Inter-ethnic prejudice is a problem too. Some interviewees claim that this is getting worse.

> 'Yes, it is becoming worse. Not just with English people but even Muslim, Sikh, Hindu, and West Indian are picking on each other.'
>
> *Sikh man*

> 'Most people hate blacks.'
>
> *Sikh man*

> 'I just don't like them [black people]
>
> *Jewish woman*

> 'My dad is a racist, but he hasn't forced his views on me.'
>
> *Black man*

If the underlying belief was that the law would *transform* attitudes, this has palpably not happened. It could, arguably, even have had the opposite effect because the need for these measures have never properly been 'sold' to the public. The IPPR survey found that nearly a fifth of white British people resent the law because it gives ethnic minorities 'special treatment.'

Local interviews

Following this general research the IPPR conducted some interviews in two London boroughs.

Somerstown

A detailed qualitative study was carried out by the author for six weeks in Somerstown, in the London Borough of Camden from June to December 1995. A young white schoolboy had been killed by a group of Bangladeshi boys in August 1994 and tensions had been high between the disenfranchised white and Bangladeshi populations since then. This area was therefore not chosen because it was representative but to find out more about attitudes in an area in which racial tension was known to be high.

Sixty white people were interviewed from June to September 1995. Twenty were women. The age range was 18-59. Half of the men and most of the women were unemployed. Among those employed, a number worked in the public sector in low paid jobs. Some were self-employed traders or manual workers. All lived in public housing.

None of those interviewed said that they had any friends among their Bangladeshi neighbours. Asked how they would describe the Asians, the five most common words were: 'scroungers', 'dirty', 'animals', 'pigs' and 'not British'. The most common opinion expressed was that they 'lived off the state' and that the council gave them everything while neglecting the white community. Only two people said that they thought Bangladeshis suffered racism. Ten said that the Bangladeshis invented stories about racial harassment. The rest said that they brought it on themselves by their 'unacceptable behaviour'.

Five people said that the only good thing that they had contributed to the country was Indian food. All but fifteen of those interviewed said that they should be 'sent back' and 20 people said that they would vote for a party which was ready to protect white interests. Thirteen white men said that they would use violence against 'Pakis'. Five said that they had been in violent encounters. Three advocated forced sterilisation for Asians and one went as far as saying that if 'these people' had more than two children, they should be forced to have abortions or lose their benefits. As far as it was possible to assess, none of those interviewees had connections with any extremist groups.

Thirty Bangladeshis were also interviewed from September to December 1995. Ten were women and the age range was 18-59. Ten of the Bangladeshis said that no one in their family had a job. Among the rest, the men worked in low paid jobs in restaurants, shops or market stalls. Only one person said he had a white colleague who he could describe as a friend. The most common words used about the white community were: 'selfish', 'bad', 'prejudiced', and 'no respect'. Twenty three of those interviewed claimed that they were discriminated against and verbally abused regularly. Eight young men said that they would retaliate with physical force if they were provoked and that they hated 'these whites'. Five said that they had physically attacked white boys and would do so again. Most of the women said that they were afraid of white people and would not let their children play with white children in the streets. Amongst those who had been brought up in the UK, most said that they wished their parents had not come to this country.

Anthropologist Rosemary Harris who carried out her own research in the area before and after the time of the murder found similar levels of inter-ethnic tensions in the area and concluded that these were linked to structural problems like high unemployment and poverty.[92]

London Boroughs of Richmond and Hounslow

For contrast, qualitative interviews were also carried out on one housing estate (in Richmond) and on a street in Hounslow (both within London) where the houses are mainly privately owned. The interviews were carried out in between Dec-March 1995/96 and the areas were selected because it is multiracial and suburban. Thirty families were interviewed.

In both neighbourhoods, there were several examples of white families who thought that black people should be sent home and that refugees were simply illegal immigrants. A typical comment was: 'This is our country and they just come to get benefits. We should get rid of them. The politicians do nothing so we let the Pakis know that they are not wanted.' Ten sets of parents said that they would not let their children play with the 'Pakis' and the children expressed similar views. There was evidence that some black and Asian families had developed a hatred for white people, saying that they did not wish to have anything to do with them. Young Asians and blacks, many brought up here, were the most vocal proponents of separatism. Two teenagers, one Asian and one black, said they had been ostracised for going out with white girls. One had been seriously assaulted.

Political leadership

For government to create a more racially harmonious society, the findings of these surveys suggest that political leaders do not only need to address discriminatory behaviour but address the attitudes which lie behind it – directly. This was recognised as long ago as the 1960s. In their monumental study, *Colour and Citizenship*, Jim Rose and Nicholas Deakin found that the degree of prejudice against people of colour was 'considerable' but that the degree of tolerance was 'even greater.' They concluded that:

> the extent of basic inclination towards tolerance suggests strongly that forthright unequivocating leadership would be a powerful factor in allaying unfounded anxieties... Conversely there is a danger that in the absence of leadership, anyone who wishes to play upon the anxieties of the majority, who lie between the extremes of tolerance and hostility can move them towards prejudiced attitudes.[93]

and in 1968, Dipak Nandy, then the Director of the Runnymede Trust said:

> It is the duty of politicians to heed popular opinion. It is equally the duty of politicians to educate public opinion. But nothing in the theory of democratic politics requires politicians to give way to popular prejudices, especially where the rights of the minorities are at stake.[94]

The challenge of forthright, unequivocating leadership in allaying unfounded anxieties was not taken up to the regret, now, of commentators like Michael Ignatieff:

> It is an invariable rule of European politics to think the worst of voters. Yet racial attitudes, since they are an unstable mix of fears and fantasies, are especially susceptible to changes in the public culture. They are not a set of atavistic facts ... before which all politicians must kneel. Racial attitudes can be changed. Witness how far British racial attitudes have changed since Powell's river of blood speech. Yet today few European politicians imagine they can lead or shape racial opinion, still less nail prejudice for what it is.[95]

The last thirty years have not only witnessed a failure to address those fears and fantasies. Politicians have, in may instances, fuelled those fears. The historical legacy which today's politicians have to address, set out in the next chapter, is one in which politicians focused public hostility first on immigrants and then on asylum seekers, failing to acknowledge the inevitable impact which this would have on attitudes towards minorities already settled in the UK. Paddy Ashdown MP, Leader of The Liberal Democrats:

> Thirty to forty years ago, Britain was essentially an all white society. Today, especially in the major centres of population, it is quite clear that our society is multiracial and equally evident that the change is a permanent one. This has been a relatively rapid transition. Many people however have been slow to come to terms with it. The result has been racial and religious prejudice, narrow nationalism, and most obviously fear of loss of national identity... The prime responsibility for changing political cultures lies with political leaders... Racial attacks do not happen in a vacuum. They occur within a political system in which immigration and asylum policies are based upon the assumption that people from different cultures are a 'problem'.[96]

The challenge of social transformation

Changing attitudes in this area is a substantial task and one that should have been initiated by political leaders as post war immigration gathered pace. Societies experiencing such demographic and cultural shifts cannot simply be expected to change perceptions, especially if the political leadership gives out contradictory messages on the consequences of those changes. Professor Bhikhu Parekh:

> Like individuals, societies go about their business in a largely unselfconscious manner. They are generally well-adjusted to their environment and have adequate resources to deal with the such problems they face. A difficult situation arises when they are confronted with unusual problems and painful choices, or when their environment undergoes rapid and extensive changes, or when their way of life faces unexpected internal or external threats. Their horizon of expectations is then disturbed, their habitual assumptions about their social world are challenged and the tacit self- understanding upon which they normally rely becomes proves inadequate. [97]

Immigration is not the only issue on which successive governments have left the public to adjust to new social and economic realities causing profound misgivings, instead of taking a proactive role of informing the public to assuage their anxieties. The most obvious example is the establishment of closer ties with Europe. As with race policies, integration with Europe has not been managed well. It has added a new dimension for many Britons worried about the nature of the country in which they live. Public education and information rarely keep up with new developments in Europe. The Demos report, *Europe: The Search for European Identity* shows not only how little popular support there is for the EU but also that that lack of support is due, in part, to the failure of political leaders to make the public aware of the benefits of EU membership.[98] As in relation to race, public opinion has been formed in this area less by facts than by the perceptions and the political rhetoric of vocal proponents or opponents. The media often takes the lead and politicians have followed the ensuing public mood rather than the other way around.[99]

This adaptation to the reality of a multi-cultural Britain was never going to be easy for a population which had for decades imbibed beliefs about Britain's imperial superiority. But the messages which Britain's political leaders have sent to the public since the Empire Windrush arrived in 1948, set out in the next chapter, bear a considerable responsibility for the failure to create the cohesive, inclusive multi-racial society which they are seeking.

3. The historical legacy

It is clear from the evidence set out in the previous chapter that racial prejudice is present in British society at an unacceptably high level. Such prejudice is not 'natural' and is causing antagonism and anxiety among all racial, ethnic and religious groups. Like most intractable problems, its roots lie in history. Although new agendas, approaches and alignments develop over time, the assumptions set down in previous decades on this issue continue to dominate discourse and the process of modernisation has yet to happen.

This chapter examines the responses of British politicians and the public to post-war immigration and towards settled minorities, tracing key events which influenced public opinion.

1948-1958: Post War immigration

It was on 22 June 1948 that the Empire Windrush landed at Tilbury, carrying 492 Jamaicans, the first batch of post-war immigrants to this country from the Caribbean. Many of these men and women had served here in the Second World War and the headline in the *Evening Standard* on that day was: 'Welcome Home'.[100] In his seminal book on the history of black immigration, *Staying Power*, Peter Fryer was of the opinion that:

> Officialdom at both government and local levels moved swiftly to make the Jamaicans feel welcome and find them accommodation and work.[101]

Indeed the Conservative Sir David Maxwell Fyfe said in that year:

> We are proud that we impose no colour bar restrictions. We must maintain our great metropolitan tradition of hospitality to everyone from every part of our Empire.[102]

These sentiments were an extension of imperial ambition and enterprise, but they were also an important demonstration of the positive leadership which was attempting to influence the attitudes of the general population towards the early immigrants. Unfortunately, this welcome was only a part of the story. When the Windrush landed, politicians were already discussing the 'problems' these immigrants would create for the British nation. Eleven Labour MPs wrote to Prime Minister Clement Attlee expressing their concerns in the stark terms which framed the debates that were to come:

> An influx of coloured people domiciled here is likely to impair the harmony, strength and cohesion of our public and social life and cause discord and unhappiness among all concerned.[103]

Attlee responded by saying that, if unrestricted immigration resulted in 'a great influx of undesirables', action would be taken to control the flow. [104]

In this exchange, 'are contained many of the assumptions that have shaped both official and popular attitudes to post-war immigration.'[105] At the very point of arrival, black people were seen as potential agents of social friction, immigration was perceived as a potential threat to good race relations and those arriving were represented not as an asset but as a burden. In contrast, white immigration to the United States and Canada, which had escalated after the war, was described mostly in affirmative terms. Record numbers of British citizens emigrated to Canada and were welcomed and accorded full rights.[106]

Continuing ambiguities

Within all of the political parties, there was a wide spectrum of opinion ranging from hostility to black immigration to a sense of obligation to British subjects and a concern for the practical realities confronting post war Britain. In 1951 the Conservatives came to power and Cabinet papers of the time reveal that Churchill and Eden had anxieties about the consequences of black immigration but that they neither wanted to jeopardise the relationship that Britain had with the ex-colonies nor cut off the supply of low paid labour. The Macmillan government, through the late fifties, regarded immigration as essential to rebuild the national economy. But they were also fearful of the 'colour problem' in the United States and many did themselves harbour prejudiced attitudes.[107] The Cabinet papers for 1955 illustrate how racial attitudes formed the foundation of early immigration control. Alec Douglas-Home:

> On the one hand it would presumably be politically
> impossible to legislate for a colour bar and any legislation
> would have to be non-discriminatory in form ... [But] we do
> not wish to keep out immigrants of good type from the old
> dominions ... I understand that ... immigration officers could,
> without giving rise to trouble or publicity, exercise such a
> measure of discrimination as we think desirable.[108]

Political leadership and popular responses to immigration

The ambiguity in the views expressed by political leaders was reflected
in those of ordinary people.

Some of the earliest research into attitudes was carried out by
Anthony Richmond in 1954, followed by Michael Banton who
conducted a survey in 1956, the results of which were published in
White and Coloured in 1959.[109] Richmond found that the population
could be split into three with one-third being 'tolerant' of coloured
people, one-third being 'mildly prejudiced' and one-third being
'extremely prejudiced'. He found that there was a tendency among
white Britons to emphasise the 'backwardness' of 'coloured' people but
that there was little deep seated racial hostility.[110]

Following his own research, Banton questioned whether
Richmond's descriptions of attitudes did not *underestimate* the degree of
tolerance which existed at the time. Banton found some 10 per cent of
respondents rigidly adhered to the belief that 'coloured people' were
culturally inferior[111] but that, although the rest held stereotypical views
of black people, these were not entrenched and had not become 'articles
of faith'. He found high levels of tolerance and concluded that the
discrimination which undoubtedly existed was often the result of the
uncertainty created by debates about immigration. Gallup carried out a
survey in the same year and was then responsible for several further
polls on white attitudes on several race related issues over the next ten
years. The Gallup evidence was re-analysed by Ruth Glass who found
that young women were the most tolerant group while young men were
the least tolerant. Glass also found that the greatest incidence of
intolerance was in the Midlands.[112]

That inconsistency encouraged researchers and commentators to conclude that public attitudes were not inflexible nor necessarily negative. Anthony Richmond, who himself shared the views expressed by the anti-immigration Labour MPs, reached the conclusion that race relations in Britain were 'fluid in character and susceptible to education and modifications'.[113]

Paul Foot in one of the most authoritative accounts of this period of early settlement observed:

> In the predominantly working class areas where the immigrants have settled they have encountered two contradictory reactions – on the one hand decency, hospitality and solidarity; on the other, resentment and xenophobia.[114]

Foot was also convinced that there was enough goodwill, and a lack of hardened conviction, which could have been built upon by the leadership:

> Commonwealth immigrants in Britain, before they became the playthings of party politics, and despite a total lack of Government concern and planning, were greeted with general friendliness and hospitality. Of course there was a colour bar in some pubs. Of course there was antagonism in some factories and bus garages. But these were exceptions. Overall the reaction was kind, even helpful. A considerate and co-ordinated effort by politicians to assist assimilation, to isolate and punish the racialist minority would have been decisive.[115]

It is important, however, not to underestimate the overt racism that prevailed in this country. As early as 1948, incidents of racial disturbances were recorded. In Liverpool hundreds were involved in mob violence and racial attacks.[116] Similar scenes took place in Deptford a year later and in 1954 there were two days of violence in North London.[117]

Nor should the goodwill be overstated. White trade unionists resisted the entry and promotion of black and Asian workers[118] and some writers take the view that, where black workers were welcomed, it was only because of the low cost labour which private and public employers could exploit at will.[119] In many areas immigrants were not regarded as a threat because they took up the poorly paid jobs that white working class people did not want to do. This was of course the period when Enoch Powell himself, as the Minister of Health, encouraged the recruitment of overseas nurses, doctors and ancillary workers to work in the expanding National Health Service. So powerful was this economic imperative that, when he met members of the newly formed British Immigration Control association, he declined to support their views.[120]

What is indisputable is that the public responses to this early phase of settlement were complex but not fixed. Nevertheless, the 1950 Cabinet papers revealed that the Labour government did not believe that public education would reduce white prejudice.[121] That historical moment of real opportunity to set the tone of public debate was all too brief, and the much needed process of planned integration was neglected. Layton Henry:

> The response to colonial migration to Britain by politicians and policy makers in the 1950s was hesitant and ambiguous and little positive was done to assist their settlement, integration and acceptance... It was not welcomed as a response to manpower needs and a valuable asset in creating economic growth and sustaining higher living standards and prosperity... A more positive early lead by government and political leaders might have done much to assuage public anxieties.[122]

In order to discover for ourselves how people responded to the first waves of large scale immigration we interviewed fifty white pensioners in London and Birmingham, exploring their perceptions of immigrants in the fifties and early sixties. The interviewees were all people who had worked alongside black and Asian Britons either in the private or public sector and who had therefore developed close working relationships with ethnic minority individuals. We found criticism that little responsibility was taken by the governments then to educate people about immigration. A seventy year old ex-railway worker told us:

We believed we were better than blacks and that is why we had the right to rule them. Then they arrived to work with us on the railways. They were good men, but you could never forget what you learnt all your life about them, that they could never be as good as white men. They came to live next to us. We were just expected to live with that. They [the government] never asked us how we felt. I am not saying we should not have let them in, no Ma'am. My grandchild is half Jamaican and he's family. But our feelings were ignored as they are now.[123]

Zig Layton-Henry believes politicians needed to tell the public that:

Immigration has contributed to economic growth and prosperity. It has acted as a check on inflation as migrant workers have been prepared to work long hours for low wages. They have also assisted in the upward social and economic mobility of indigenous British workers because, as a replacement labour force, they have been assigned the lowest positions in the labour and housing markets.[124]

This did not happen. Politicians of all parties began to play the race card more openly as immigration continued not only from the West Indies, but also from India and Pakistan. Labour needs in Britain remained acute. Immigrant factory workers were asked by employers to bring in their family and friends, if necessary from the subcontinent.[125] But in spite of the fact that their labour was required, throughout the late Fifties and through the Sixties, black and Asian immigrants were increasingly to experience overt racial antagonism.[126]

At a personal level, social mingling between black men and white women was common in urban areas. The 1958 race riots were partly triggered by the distaste felt by many white men that this should be happening.[127]

1958 riots and the political response

In September 1958, violence erupted in Nottingham and in North Kensington. Over six thousand white people were involved and the tensions and attacks on black people lasted for days. The Prime Minister of Jamaica was sufficiently concerned to fly to London. Lord Justice Salmon said later that the attackers had brought shame on the areas affected and that their actions had 'filled the whole nation with horror'.[128] Although the violence was condemned, many politicians argued that the riots were a symptom of genuine anxieties felt by white Britons about 'coloured' immigration, and the solution therefore lay in stricter immigration controls. Conservative and Labour MPs in Nottingham immediately called for a halt to all 'coloured' immigration. Alec Douglas-Home, then Minister of State for Commonwealth Relations, put forward the same view. Immigration control and 'good race relations' had become one.[129]

A poll carried out for *The Daily Express* in the immediate aftermath of the riots showed 80 per cent of white Britons in support of immigration controls.[130] Many in the Labour party, however, appalled at the racial violence directed at black people, took a position of total opposition to immigration controls and the NEC declared its intention to introduce anti-discrimination legislation.[131] This, speculates Layton-Henry, may have been a miscalculation:

> ... they were unable to see that the strength of public opinion on coloured immigration would have to be appeased... [The riots] ... seem to have prevented the Labour Party from developing a realistic policy on immigration policy which would have both reassured the public about the size and consequences of New Commonwealth immigration and at the same time been non-racist. The riots were regarded as ugly isolated incidents and not part of a rising trend of opposition to black immigration which might have growing political significance. [132]

Meanwhile, some Conservative politicians stepped up a vocal campaign to keep out 'coloured' immigrants, asking whether it made sense to turn Britain into a multi-racial community. Foot argued that such politicians had a particularly damaging effect on race relations:

> With no other issue are the attitudes struck by politicians more crucial. In the choice of economic priorities, the level of

social services, the character of defence, the politicians play a minor role. The big decisions are made for them by civil servants, managing directors and the international rate of exchange. So irrational is race and colour propaganda that its exploitation by politicians has an effect proportionately far wider than political propaganda on other matters... Even conditions of substantial unemployment and poverty, though capable of provoking race resentment and antagonism are unlikely to do as much damage to race relations as are the rantings of unscrupulous politicians.[133]

Nevertheless, in the 1959 general election, immigration was not an issue. Gallup polls between 1958 and 1961[134] showed at least one third of people interviewed either believed in free entry for immigrants or had no views on the subject. Oswald Mosley, who stood as a candidate in North Kensington, and tried to exploit the feelings of white people in the area after the riots, lost his deposit.

The 10 per cent of the population that Banton had found to be most hostile to 'coloured people' in his research in 1956 were again identified in a localised survey carried out in the London Borough of Willesden a few months after the 1958 'race' riots. A grant from the local authority funded a survey to establish the attitudes of the white population towards ethnic minorities who had emigrated to the area. The survey found that 10 per cent of the community were 'highly prejudiced'.[135]

The Sixties

In the 1960s, this somewhat contradictory picture and political vacillation continued, as race relations deteriorated in some respects and improved in others. In relation to immigration, public opinion (whether real or imagined) led politicians in a manner untypical for the rest of British politics:

There was a decline in the beneficent liberal spirit within middle opinion itself and 'race relations' became not the means of a confident promotion of policies of multi-racial harmony ... but an increasingly defensive assertion of liberal values on race which had formerly been attached to the Commonwealth idea

but which were cut adrift on a hostile sea and on a boat with no
clear instructions as to where it was to navigate to. [136]

The emotional fallout of decolonisation cannot be underestimated; its
effects on white public confidence and attitudes were deep and long
lasting. The vacuum created by the end of imperial dreams (which the
Commonwealth concept could in no real way replace), and the racial
antagonism manifest from some sections of the population, made space
for the introduction of immigration controls aimed at those from the
Commonwealth and eventually for Powellism, arguably one of the most
damaging developments for race relations since the war.

The Commonwealth Immigrants Act 1962

At the Conservative party conference in 1961, thirty nine resolutions
demanded restrictions on immigration. The Commonwealth Immigrants
Bill was subsequently published and had considerable public support.
Commonwealth citizens born in the UK and those with passports issued
by the UK government could enter the country freely. All others had to
apply for Ministry of Labour vouchers. The long tradition of treating all
Commonwealth people as British subjects with equal rights of
citizenship ended with that Act. That racial exclusion was the real aim
of the 1962 Act is accepted by William Deedes who was Minister
without Portfolio at the time:

> The Bill's real purpose was to restrict the influx of coloured
> immigrants. We were reluctant to say as much openly [137]

Were politicians at this time responding to or leading public opinion?
Samit Saggar believes that the first restrictions 'did not so much follow
public sentiment as create it.'[138] Colin Brown agrees:

> The 'race relations' justification for immigration control has
> not been publicly presented by the government as an
> accommodation of white racism, however; rather, it has been
> explained in terms of problems caused by the presence of
> black immigrants. It may be that, by aiming to appease white
> opinion by turning first to immigration rather than by tackling

racialism itself, the government has nourished and given
legitimacy to anti-immigrant sentiment; thus the outcome of
the appeasement policy may have been only a deepening of
the racialist currents in British society. It is difficult to analyse
the extent to which successive immigration controls have been
responses to public opinion simply because the government's
introduction of those controls may itself have been very
influential in forming that opinion.[139]

Even during this period, however, the political leadership could and
sometimes did exert a benign influence. The fire and fury of the opposition
which greeted the Bill took the Government by surprise. Gaitskell accused
the Government of colour prejudice. The strategic onslaught by Labour
had a marked impact on public opinion, a Gallup poll finding that public
support for immigration controls fell from 76 per cent to 62 per cent.[140] In
1963 Harold Wilson spoke publicly in Trafalgar Square on the need for
public education and a change of attitudes towards immigrants. Later he
appointed a junior minister to look into the possibility of a national public
education programme and other strategies for integration. That tentative
step was not taken forward.[141]

1964 election

In the general election of 1964, Patrick Gordon-Walker, the Shadow
Foreign Secretary was defeated in Smethwick by Peter Griffiths, whose
campaign used the slogan: 'If you want a nigger neighbour, vote
Labour.' This was a turning point in British politics, says Layton-Henry,
reinforcing the politics of appeasement on immigration:

It was a shattering result and a disaster for race relations as it
appeared to show that racial prejudices could be effectively
exploited for electoral advantage. [142]

Richard Crossman who had, in 1962, condemned the Commonwealth
Immigrants Act, wrote in 1964:

Ever since the Smethwick election it has been quite clear that
immigration can be the greatest potential vote loser for the

Labour party if we are seen to be permitting a flood of
immigrants to come in and blight the central areas of our
cities.[143]

In 1965, the newly elected Labour government tightened the restrictions
on Commonwealth citizens by reducing the number of vouchers
available under the 1962 Act despite the shortage of labour. Richard
Crossman:

> We have become illiberal and lowered quotas at a time when we
> have an acute shortage of labour … nevertheless … if we had not
> done this, we would have been faced with certain electoral defeat
> in the West Midlands and South East. Politically, fear of
> immigration is the most powerful undertow today.[144]

Race Relations Act, 1965

By 1965, a bipartisan consensus had emerged: stricter immigration
controls were to be matched by measures to ensure fair treatment for
immigrants and minorities who settled in the UK. The 1965 Race
Relations Act outlawed discrimination in specified public places like
cinemas and transport facilities and made it illegal for anyone to publish
or distribute written matter which deliberately stirred up racial hatred. A
Race Relations Board was set up to deal with complaints but housing
and employment were not covered. The spirit of this law was
conciliatory; it urged people to do what was right rather than imposing
punitive measures.

One year later, a major study by Political and Economic Planning
(PEP) revealed that direct discrimination against ethnic minorities was
still commonplace. It found that employers and house owners were
denying black and Asian people jobs and accommodation on the basis
of their own racial prejudices. [145] Nevertheless, many liberals felt that
race relations were still capable of being influenced positively. In *Colour
and Citizenship*, a significant study which drew on extensive survey
evidence (see below), Jim Rose and Nicholas Deakin concluded:

> A forthright, unequivocating leadership would be a powerful
> factor in allaying unfounded anxieties. Conversely there is a

danger that in the absence of leadership, anyone who wishes to play on the anxieties of the majority ... can move them towards prejudiced attitudes.[146]

Commonwealth Immigrants Act, 1968

Immigration again became a major political issue in 1968 as British Asians in East Africa came under pressure after independence. Africanisation policies of the Kenyan Government caused many of Asians to leave Kenya and come to Britain to settle. As British passport holders they were free to enter under the 1962 Act. Enoch Powell and others were making increasingly vociferous anti-immigration speeches. The Government panicked and rushed through a Bill imposing strict quotas and removing automatic entry to people with British passports, except those born here or descended from a British parent or grandparent. It was seen by many as a betrayal of principle and of a community who had retained their British citizenship in good faith. The vigour with which Labour took up the politics of appeasement was condemned by Auberon Waugh who described the new measures as 'the most immoral pieces of legislation ever to have emerged from any British parliament.'[147]

1968 Race Relations Act

It was in part to counter criticism of its immigration policy that the Government introduced the 1968 Race Relations Act. In 1976 Liberal MP Alan Beith said that the first two Race Relations Acts were a 'counter balance or accompaniment to new legislation restricting immigration', and that it was wrong 'that the two things should be as closely associated as this created suspicion and anxiety.'[148] The Act made it unlawful to discriminate on grounds of colour, race, ethnic or national origins in housing, employment, and the provision of services. Displays of discriminatory notices were made unlawful and the Race Relations Board was given powers to investigate cases if there were grounds to suspect that discrimination had taken place even if no complaint had been received.

The emphasis was still on conciliation with legal redress seen as a last resort. The Community Relations Commission was set up with responsibility to promote good race relations. But even as the Bill was going through Parliament, there was concern that good race relations could not be promoted in the atmosphere of public hostility against New Commonwealth immigration which had been encouraged by the recent debate on the strengthening of immigration controls.[149] Some politicians were also concerned that public support for the new Race Relations Act had not been won.[150]

Enoch Powell

1968 was also the year in which Enoch Powell made his apocalyptic speech:

> We must be mad, literally mad, as a nation, to be permitting the annual inflow of some 50,000 dependants who are for the most part the material of the future growth of the immigrant-descended population. It is like watching a nation busily engaged in heaping up its own funeral pyre... As I look ahead I am filled with foreboding. Like the Roman, I seem to see 'the River Tiber foaming with much blood!'[151]

The result of this speech was immediate, says Layton Henry:

> It made him the best loved and most popular member of the opposition overnight and even a serious contender for the position of leader of the party. The popular support for Powell could be measured in the polls, the deluge of favourable letters he received and the public demonstrations of support.[152]

Opinion polls showed that up to 75 per cent supported what Powell had said.[153] Later he developed his views and began to argue that the only way to sustain the nation was through repatriation because 'coloured' immigrants could never, in his eyes, be Englishmen.[154] He also planted the seeds of suspicion among the white British population claiming that the political elite did not understand them and were hiding immigration facts from the rest of the population. Two decades later, in 1995, Charles Wardle MP resigned as Immigration Minister and fed the same fears when he claimed that the public were not being given the information about how many 'millions' of people would come into this country if European Union internal border controls were scrapped.[155]

Public opinion

The aim of the *Colour and Citizenship* seminal study was 'to measure the incidence of colour prejudice in the white population, the demographic characteristics of those who could be described as highly prejudiced and the psychological traits which differentiate prejudiced from non-prejudiced people.'[156] Over two and a half thousand people were interviewed between December 1966 and April 1997.

Four 'types' of people emerged from the research. They were:

Tolerant	30-40%
Tolerant-inclined	34-42%
Prejudiced inclined	12-20%
Prejudiced	6-14%

Nearly a third of those interviewed expressed no trace of prejudice towards ethnic minorities and another two fifths seemed 'strongly disposed in the direction of tolerance'. Ten per cent were unconditionally hostile and one sixth were hostile but prepared to make some exceptions.

Other key findings included the following:

● Women were slightly more tolerant than men.

● Extreme prejudice was most likely among the 45-54 year skilled manual workers and their wives and least likely among the professional classes and unskilled and semi-skilled workers. It was least apparent among the young and elderly populations. This last fact has now changed markedly as it is often the elderly who now display some of the most negative attitudes. These people would have been in the younger age band in the 1960s.

● The highest levels of prejudice were found among those in the lower middle classes.

● People who voted Conservative were more prejudiced than Labour voters and still more prejudiced than Liberals. But the figures were close. 30 per cent of Conservative voters were either

prejudiced or inclined to prejudice. The figure for Labour voters
was 26 per cent and Liberals 20 per cent.

- Among the tolerant groups there was little significant difference
  between the working classes and the middle classes.

- There was little evidence to support the view that people who
  had travelled overseas were less prejudiced than those who had
  not.

- Nearly 60 per cent of people interviewed felt optimistic about the
  future. Such a high rating does not appear with much frequency
  now, although the British Social Attitudes Surveys have had
  some 'good' years.

- People who were more 'authoritarian' in relation to other issues,
  were substantially more prejudiced than those with more liberal
  views. Eurobarometer studies confirm that there is still a strong
  correlation.

- 60 per cent or more of the respondents thought that ethnic
  minorities took more out of the country than they put in. The
  figure in Wolverhampton, Enoch Powell's constituency, was 75
  per cent. The percentage concerned with white immigrants was
  significantly lower.

- Stereotypes that were common included beliefs that ethnic
  minorities brought dirt, diseases and overcrowding, and that
  they were responsible for neighbourhood decline.

- Only ten per cent of those interviewed were hostile to those
  minorities who were British by birth. Today, immigrants and
  British born ethnic minorities are not so clearly distinguished in
  the minds of the white public.

- The three main fears expressed about ethnic minorities in Britain
  were that they would have a bad effect on the neighbourhood
  (31 per cent), that they would intermarry with whites (25 per
  cent) and that they would become the majority (22 per cent).

The study also concluded:

It is often argued that fears of being 'swamped' by what is described as a 'flood' of migrants is a key element in forming attitudes, and that this derives from exaggerated notions of the extent of the migration and the size of the coloured population (which are compounded by the absence of reliable official statistics). By and large, our results support the view that exaggerated estimates are in circulation.[157]

Comparing this with the recent research findings set out in Chapter 2, we can see that there have been some improvements. But many negative attitudes, preoccupations, fears and the language of 'swamping' and 'flooding' persist. The percentage of people inclined towards tolerance in the 1960s was much higher than in some of the later surveys in the 1990s.

Colour and Citizenship also compared attitudes as measured by other researchers, and their own, over the ten year period from 1958-68.

Table 3.1 – Survey evidence on public attitudes to immigration control, 1958-1968

What kind of immigration policy?

	1958*	1958	1961 May	1961 Oct	1961 Nov	1963	1964	1965	1968 Mar	1968 Apr	1968 Apr**
Free entry	37	21	21	12	21	19	10	5	6	3	1
Control	53	65	73	76	62	70	88	88	90	91	95
Don't know	10	14	6	12	17	11	2	7	4	6	3

All figures were taken from Gallup surveys, except *Banton.
1965 and Mar 1968 survey question was 'Do you agree with proposals for further control?'
Apr 1968 survey question was 'Are controls too stringent?',** Apr 1968 after the Enoch Powell speech.
Source: *Colour and Citizenship*, Table 28.24

Table 3.2 – Survey evidence on public attitudes to race relations, 1964-1968

Is the situation getting better or worse?

	1964 Aug	1965 Nov	1965 Dec	1966 Jan	1967 Aug	1968 Apr
Better	24	14	18	19	13	6
Worse	26	43	39	33	45	55
Same	41	31	33	37	33	32
Don't Know	9	12	10	11	9	7

All figures were taken from Gallup surveys.
Source: *Colour and Citizenship*, Table 28.24

Comparing some of the poll findings a decade apart produces some important evidence of how attitudes were altering. In 1958 29 per cent of people interviewed said they would mind working with a 'coloured' man. By 1968 the figure had dropped to 19 per cent. But when asked if they would move if 'coloured' people moved next door, 9 per cent said they would in 1958 but 19 per cent said they would a decade later. In 1958 70 per cent said they would *not* move, but by 1968 that figure had fallen to 31 per cent. Eighty per cent in both surveys said that they did not object to 'coloured' children at their child's school.

Politicians manifestly had an impact on attitudes. Gallup carried out surveys before and after Enoch Powell's speech in April 1968 and found that in early April, only 29 per cent of respondents objected to legislation against discrimination. By the end of that month the figure jumped to 46 per cent with only 30 per cent of respondents positively stating that there should be legislation against discrimination.

The Seventies

Tony Benn's entry in his diary for 16 January 1974 reports that Harold Wilson instructed Labour politicians to 'ignore Enoch Powell, because last time the attack on him lost five seats.'[158]

Layton Henry:

> the Government was on the defensive, desperately trying to hold the bipartisan consensus against the onslaughts of Enoch Powell and his friends with Edward Heath trailing behind Powell but gradually moving the conservative policies towards tougher and tougher controls.[159]

Leaders were acting as followers. Conservatives first and then Labour made themselves hostages to (often ill informed) public opinion instead of influencing opinion to back policies which would improve race relations and benefit the country. Although there was no love lost between Heath and Powell, public opinion had been ignited by the latter and been placated by the Conservative victory. This happened even though only a quarter of the Conservative candidates took up the issue of race and immigration during their campaigns. They were still perceived to be tougher on immigration.

1971 Immigration Act and the Ugandan Asian crisis

The 1971 Immigration Act replaced employment vouchers with work permits which did not give people rights of permanent residence nor entry rights to dependants. People who were connected by birth or descent to the United Kingdom were free to enter. The rights of non-white Commonwealth citizens to settle in Britain effectively ended with this Act. It helped to confirm the feeling that the Conservative Government could be trusted to keep tight immigration controls.

This belief was to be shattered in 1972 with the Ugandan crisis. In August of that year Idi Amin announced the expulsion of the 50,000 Asians who had lived in the country for generations. The majority of them had British passports. This tested the reputation that Heath had established. Was he now going to be tough enough to reject calls to take responsibility for these Citizens? Enoch Powell, the Monday Club and the National Front reacted with predictable hostility and insisted that the United Kingdom had no moral case to take in the dispossessed Asians. Ordinary Britons and local authorities also indicated that they would not be prepared to admit the thousands who were affected by Amin's order. Local authorities in Leicester and Ealing paid for advertisements in newspapers asking Ugandan Asians not to move into their areas.

The government nevertheless decided to honour the UK's obligations and accept its Citizens who were being threatened by a dictator with incarceration in concentration camps. This position was not adopted until Heath had tried to get other countries to 'share the burden'[160] a stance which contributed to the poor presentation of the decision to the public. That decision could have been presented as a conscientious leader making an honourable, moral decision. The Ugandan Asians were educated, skilled people who would become an asset to this country and Heath did eventually adopt this line. Uganda's loss was 'our' gain he said and, to his credit, he made resources available to enable successful integration. But by this time negative attitudes towards the Ugandan Asians had already taken hold.

Race Relations Act 1976

By the mid-Seventies it had become clear that there was a need for a tighter and more effective Race Relations Act. The 1968 Act was not respected by most black people and surveys by the PEP confirmed that, although direct discrimination had been reduced, indirect discrimination was a significant factor in the social exclusion of racial minorities.[161] The Home Office produced a White Paper on racial disadvantage which recommended a 'fuller strategy' to combat discrimination and to ensure genuine equal opportunities for young black and Asian Britons born in the UK. Roy Jenkins, when he introduced the Bill, said that racism was morally repugnant and that the success of the legislation depended on political leadership and the attitudes of society. Conservative MP Sir George Sinclair spoke in equally powerful terms about the Race Relations Acts and why they were important:

> Those of us, who, on both sides of this House, supported those Acts hoped that by the bringing to an end of a wide range of discriminatory practices, attitudes would also change. It is one of the great myths that laws do not change attitudes.[162]

Under the 1976 Act, discriminatory cases could be now taken to the county court or in the case of employment, to industrial tribunals. Legal definitions of discrimination were extended to cover organisational practices as well as individual behaviour. Indirect discrimination was made unlawful.

The Commission For Racial Equality was established by the Act, in part to:

> inform and educate public opinion on race relations... [There is a case for] the general education of society about the need to regard ourselves as a multiracial society and to act accordingly.[163]

In practice, successive governments have relied on the CRE to undertake all necessary promotional work, not recognising that the government itself must be seen to be taking the lead.[164]

During the 1970s, extreme right wing parties made substantial gains in recruitment and electoral victories. In the 1976 local elections, in Deptford the National Front and the National Party between them captured nearly 44 per cent of the votes. This was, Samit Saggar believes because:

The period between the mid Seventies and the early Eighties witnessed an intense rise in domestic anti-immigration political sentiment.[165]

There were people who felt that political leaders were 'betraying' the white population. Little was done to counter the scare mongering and other disturbing developments. John Twitchin:

> ... the result of ignorance of the facts, rationalised by the 'leave well alone' approach, has been to leave the stage clear for those who, wittingly or otherwise, speak and act on racist assumptions to take the initiative both in public opinion leadership and in setting the agenda of public discussion.[166]

Margaret Thatcher, who became leader of the Conservative party in 1975, had been among the forty four Conservatives who were opposed to the 1976 Race Relations Act. [167] In 1978 on *World In Action*, Mrs Thatcher justified cultural xenophobia by saying that she understood the British people's fear 'that this country might be rather swamped by people with a different culture.'[168] In this statement lie the roots of what was to come later: her own, deeply felt, peculiarly white and nationalistic version of Britishness and her rejection of the ideology of multiculturalism. Many saw her as an honest politician unafraid to articulate what the ordinary white population was feeling and departing from the elitist liberal consensus which had ignored and misled these people on immigration. The party's ratings rose by nine per cent in the immediate aftermath of the programme. Saggar:

> From 1976, the apparently orchestrated strategy was employed by the Conservative leadership to alter public perceptions of the party's position on immigration. Interpretations of these strategic moves however vary from those of supporters who emphasised the need to bring public opinion and policy commitments back into line to those of critics who asserted that it merely pandered to crude racism.[169]

This was a period when a twin track approach to voters was astutely developed. White voters anxious about immigration were placated;

black voters in key areas were told that they were indispensable to the country and part of the Thatcher dream. The famous poster used by the Conservatives with a smart black man and a slogan saying 'Labour says he is black; Tories say he is British' was but one example.

The Eighties

The 1980s were, for the most part, the era of strong leadership driving the nation with right wing, free market conviction politics. Margaret Thatcher developed further her neo-Powellite view on English nationhood and British history which appealed to many in the white British population. She was determined to put back the 'great' in Britain and this included pride in the Empire. She made this clear in her Bruges speech in 1991, when she asked her people to be proud that they had conquered and civilised the rest of the world.[170] Philip Dodd:

> Mrs Thatcher's Britishness depended ... upon a sustained process of purification and exclusion. In her British story, enemies were here, there and everywhere... Mrs Thatcher hardly invented such a strategy since Britishness has long worked on the principle of separating the inside sheep from the outside goats. Sometimes they have been Catholics, denied the vote, other times they have been Jewish people, and more recently people from the Caribbean or Asia. While the groups may change the principle does not – their presence threatens the historic identity of Britain.[171]

When Prime Minister Thatcher felt compelled to admit Vietnamese refugees to the UK in the 1980s, and to provide resources for their settlement, her government did present their arrival positively to win public support, focusing on the generosity of the British people and the skills of the refugees.

During the 1980s, equal opportunity policies were implemented by many local authorities to transform the racial composition of their workforce and to realise the obligations which they had under Section 71 of the Race Relations Act: to 'make the appropriate arrangements ... to promote equality of opportunity' and 'good relations between people of different racial groups.' After the 1981 riots and the Scarman Report which followed, the Greater London Council (GLC) and the Inner London Education Authority (ILEA) also took radical steps to meet those responsibilities. Some of the ideas that were implemented were ill thought out and had a detrimental effect on public opinion and on equality initiatives in general.[172] But many of the good ideas, particularly in education, were targeted for criticism because they were beginning to have an impact. In his analysis of this confrontation, Saggar observed that:

> The more scathing attacks on multiculturalism have been reserved for the progressive LEAs which have been at the forefront of innovation and reform.[173]

The Thatcher government became increasingly hostile to equalities initiatives and multiculturalism and had considerable effect on public opinion. ILEA and the GLC and some London Labour boroughs were particularly criticised by Conservatives for many of their equality initiatives. Nancy Murray:

> … what is new is the emphasis on rolling back the gains of anti-racism in the name of traditional freedoms, national pride and the liberation of the white majority.[174]

There was a unity of purpose between Downing Street, academics from right wing think tanks, the *Daily Mail*, the *Daily Telegraph* and people like Ray Honeyford, the Bradford headmaster who was sacked for publishing his views criticising multicultural education, and these cross currents of influence were undoubtedly influential.[175]

The right wing press printed articles which sometimes had no factual basis and were proved eventually to be complete fabrications . Articles which claimed that black bin-liners and 'Baa baa black sheep' were banned by 'loony' Labour councils were later shown by researchers at Goldsmith College to be untrue.[176] But the myths had entered public consciousness so effectively that in the attitudes surveys conducted in 1997 for IPPR, individuals were still claiming to be subject to this 'tyranny': 'I could get the sack for asking for black coffee' and 'They are not allowed to sing Baa Baa Black Sheep at our school.'

Inner City unrest

The eighties were also a period of serious unrest.[177] Young black Britons took to the streets in Brixton and Toxteth in 1981. These were major riots which resulted in serious injuries and substantial damage to property. Triggered by the actions of police operating in the areas, the flashpoints were signs of deeper disaffection.

Disenchantment and alienation among those who believed that they were entitled to belong, because they were British by birth, began seriously during this era. Previously, black community activists had themselves been immigrants with perhaps more limited expectations of their place in society. The Scarman Report[178] showed that there was serious material disadvantage among the black Britons in Brixton. The Policy Studies Institute reports of 1984 and 1986 (below) demonstrated that widespread discrimination persisted and that negative attitudes still prevailed towards non-white Britons.[179] The groups that were making progress (among them the Ugandan Asians with British passports) were those which had an economic base with which to start up their own businesses and buy their own homes, thereby bypassing potential discrimination by white employers and landlords.

Black and White Britain, Policy Studies Institute (1984)[180]

In 1982 PSI interviewed a national sample of 2,305 white adults and 5,001 adults of Asian and Afro-Caribbean origins. Both groups were asked a number of attitude questions, although the main aims were to measure the degree of perceived discrimination suffered by minority groups and to test the level of support for further anti-discrimination legislation. The results revealed a white English population in which the ideas of integration and anti-discrimination policy had wide support; but a population which was divided over the value of multiculturalism and said that it did not understand minority cultures:

- White people favoured integration over segregation, but a substantial minority were pessimistic about race relations problems.

- 60 per cent said that whites had now accepted people of Asian and Afro-Caribbean origins as part of British society, and nearly

90 per cent said that minorities should not keep themselves apart from white people. But 40 per cent said that problems of race relations were bound to occur when minorities and white people lived in the same area.

- Most white interviewees acknowledged the existence of racial discrimination but they held varying views on where it happened and its extent.

- Fewer than one in ten white people thought that employers or other bodies discriminated in reverse (that is, in favour of minorities) – except in the case of benefits offices and council housing departments. One in five people accused those organisations of favouring minorities.

- As regards the trend in racial discrimination, interviewees split evenly: one third said that it was increasing and one third said that it was decreasing.

- There was a surprisingly high level of support for more vigorous enforcement of anti-discrimination law and for further legislation. Half said that they agreed that the law should be enforced more effectively and over 40 per cent agreed that there should be new, stricter laws. But there was also substantial opposition: 31 per cent and 41 per cent said they disagreed with these ideas respectively.

- Three quarters said that white people did not understand minority ways of life or culture. The interviewees were evenly divided over the issue of preserving those cultures: 50 per cent agreed that minorities 'should try to preserve as much as possible', but 40 per cent disagreed.

Cultural difference, perceived lack of assimilation and the belief that ethnic minorities got preferential treatment were issues which affected white attitudes in the mid 1980s. The optimism of the 1960s was not reproduced and there was a sense that people were at best learning to adjust. But the fact that people were more aware of race discrimination and supportive of laws to combat it was also new and positive.

The Nineties

The late 1980s and 1990s were marked by a series of measures to tighten controls on immigration and on asylum seekers. The 1987 Immigration (Carriers' Liability Act) imposed fines on airlines and ferry operators bringing people into the UK without valid documents. In the debate on the future of Hong Kong's three and a half million British Dependent Territory or Overseas passport-holders, at the turn of the decade, persuasive evidence that most of those likely to come to the UK were capable of making a positive impact on the economy was ignored, politicians focusing on the perceived problems such immigrants would create for British society.[181] [182] In 1993, The Asylum and Immigration (Appeals) Act again focused public opinion on the potential problems associated with migrants when it reduced the responsibilities of local authorities to homeless asylum seekers and introduced fingerprinting for asylum seekers. The Immigration Rules 1994 further tightened the procedures for obtaining asylum.

The 1995 Immigration and Asylum Act and changes in social security legislation in 1996 resulted in further changes. Fast track appeals were introduced for asylum seekers; employers were to be charged with a criminal offence if they employed illegal immigrants and severe cuts were made in benefits for asylum seekers awaiting appeals.[183]

Impact on public opinion

The presentation of these policies was in terms of the threat posed by immigration and the need for hard measures to ensure good race relations. The 1987 Conservative Party manifesto was accompanied by a booklet outlining the major achievements of the party:

> Firm but fair immigration controls have been applied in the interest of harmonious race relations. Last year fewer people were accepted for settlement in the United Kingdom than at any time since the control of Commonwealth immigrants began in 1962.[184]

and Conservative MP Nirj Deva was one of many to adopt this argument in defending the 1995 Asylum and Immigration Bill:

> The Bill will be good for community relations. [Asians] ... are
> seen as an integral part of this county. If the Bill fails and
> bogus asylum seekers are able to be in this country, a time will
> come when everyone without strictly European features will
> be viewed as such. The destabilisation and insecurity for those
> legally settled here would have far reaching consequences. [185]

There appears, however, to have been no objective scrutiny of the
effectiveness of this dual approach in it stated aim of improving race
relations. There has been no government-backed research on the impact
of immigration laws on public attitudes, although millions of pounds
have been spent on research on other public policy issues such as
discrimination. And yet there is now a tacit understanding between the
two main political parties that strict immigration controls are essential
for racial harmony. This belief, as Keith Best of the Immigration
Advisory Service (IAS) says, ' is not based on any respectable analysis'
and detracts from the development of a rational immigration policy to
meet the needs of the country.[186] It also gives a distorted picture of
immigration into Britain. In 1997, for example, 80 per cent of those
allowed to enter and work came from Australia and New Zealand. The
IAS and the Refugee Council have initiated a campaign to influence this
debate and affect ill informed public perceptions of immigration.

There are strong grounds for suggesting that, far from reassuring
the public, the presentation of immigration policy over that period
served to heighten anxiety, not least by repeatedly identifying perceived
weaknesses in the effectiveness of immigration controls. As Sarah
Spencer has pointed out, once a government decides to:

> appease rather than to assuage public concern, new measures
> have to be proposed to show that something is being done.
> Loopholes are identified, rule changes proposed, appeal rights
> abolished, time-limits shortened, defences removed.[187]

Far from improving race relations, immigration policies and the way
they have been communicated to the public may have increased public
hostility towards immigrants and ethnic minorities because the messages
they convey are contradictory. Roy Hattersley is convinced of the
damaging effect such discourse has had and now accepts that he was

wrong to make the connection between race relations and immigration as an MP in the Sixties:

> Good community relations are not encouraged by the promotion of the idea that the entry of one more black immigrant into this country will be so damaging to the national interest that husbands must be separated from their wives, children denied the chance to look after their aged parents and sisters prevented from attending their brothers' weddings. It is measures like the Asylum and Immigration bill – and the attendant speeches – which create the impression that we cannot 'afford to let them in.' And if we cannot afford to let them in, then those of them who are already here must be ... doing harm.[188]

Hattersley's criticism is both of the substance of the policy, which targets certain categories of people, and of the messages it sends, which serves not to settle white people's anxieties but to encourage and reinforce the negative attitudes which the policies are intended to dispel. An editorial in *The Independent* asked why the then Conservative government was investing such political capital on this area:

> ... [the Home Secretary says] ... if people believed that immigration was rising too fast, then racial tension might rise. How odd then that the Government seems so assiduously to have fostered exactly this perception.[189]

The Economist similarly agreed:

> ... by promoting anti-immigration policies the government risks encouraging racism and undermining liberty. It deserves contempt, not votes, for proposing this nasty little bill.[190]

What is clear is that neither white nor black Britons have been persuaded either that we have the right immigration laws and regulations or that race relations have improved as a result of the increasingly tough measures. Nigel Harris:

> The prominent place [migration] occupies in political debate
> and the media is no testimony to the truth of the fears it
> evokes ... and the fictions which so often pass for common
> sense are allowed free rein. Constant reiteration of these
> fictions ensures that, at least for some of the time, a majority
> of people is persuaded that immigration is a serious
> problem.[191]

Sixty two per cent of white people believe that there should be less
immigration from the subcontinent and 58 per cent believe that we need
fewer immigrants from the Caribbean. If racial attitudes were supposed
to improve, how does one explain that only 30 per cent of white Britons
feel similar anxieties about white Australians?[192] Research also shows
that 30 per cent of white people believe the ethnic minority population
to be four times larger than it is[193] and that the British public
overestimates the numbers of refugees admitted into the UK.[194] Sections
of the white population act on their negative feelings At a people's
tribunal hearing in the London Borough of Hounslow on racial
harassment in February 1996, the overwhelming majority of the victims
whose personal testimonies were heard were asylum seekers.[195]

It would seem appropriate to ask, therefore, why the government
has failed to reassure the public in spite of a series of successively tighter
controls. Such questions are left unasked and the twin track policy has
in the past merely been re-asserted, without supporting evidence,
whenever new immigration and asylum legislation has been
proposed.[196]

A Survey carried out for the CRE in December 1995 showed that 79
per cent of white Britons believe that politicians exploit the issue of
immigration for political purposes.[197] Evidence that immigration has
indeed been overtly used for political purposes came from Andrew
Lansley, former head of research at Conservative Central Office who said:

> Immigration, an issue we raised successfully in 1992 and
> again in the European election campaign, played particularly
> well in the tabloids and has more potential to hurt[198]

Immigration policy has thus been used, in the past, as a political
weapon. It has proved to be a neat if predictable way of pacifying white

voters and of giving governments credibility. Tony Blair, MP then Leader of the Opposition, described the 1995 Bill as an act of appeasement and said: 'race and immigration should not be the playthings of party politics'[199] Hugo Young, writing on the same Bill:

> What it addresses is the fear of influx, which in British history and psychology is coterminous with the immigration and or asylum of non-whites. What it plays to is the evidence of private polling done by both main parties which shows that on this issue, almost alone on the political agenda, is one where the Tories score better than Labour... it presents Labour and Liberal Democrats with dilemma. For the more they denounce the Tories, the more inexorably they help the [race] card to do its venomous work.[200]

Such manoeuvres reduce the potential for a thorough analysis of the real immigration needs of the UK in terms of skills shortage, demographic predictions and other factors.[201] By failing to dislocate immigration from race relations and political expediency, governments have not been free to educate the population on immigration and refugee issues nor empowered to react assertively to the extremist mavericks within their own ranks.

Images of immigrants and refugees

The language that is used as the common currency to describe immigration and asylum has also been problematic. People who enter the country unlawfully are dehumanised by the term 'illegals' while refugees whose reason for flight falls outside of the narrow definition of a refugee under the Geneva Convention – those escaping famine or civil unrest, for example – are called 'bogus'. While many applicants for asylum are not, under international law, entitled to protection, they cannot therefore be said to be cheats and scroungers. Yet for the past few years both Conservative and Labour politicians used this obviously emotive, pejorative word for political effect. During the second reading of the Asylum and Immigration Bill in 1995, Conservative and Labour MPs used the term 'bogus' a total of 47 times.[202] Jack Straw, Shadow Home Secretary, used it when opposing the Bill, as did the Asian

Labour MP, Piara Singh Khabra, even while speaking of the dangers of such rhetoric:

> In the past I have heard many speeches on immigration, including those about rivers of blood and the swamping of British culture by foreigners. The leaders of the nation made these, and of course leaders of the Conservative party. They were used to whip up racial prejudice and to use immigration for party political purposes and they caused great damage to race relations. The present problem of bogus refugees and illegal immigrants is the creation of a Government which has been in power for sixteen years and has failed to tackle the problem.[203]

The misuse of language, and its impact, have been noticed. The Lord Bishop of Liverpool:

> I take exception to the word 'bogus'... I feel very angry when I read it in a paper like the Daily Mail. I feel even more deeply disturbed when I read in Hansard of another place the Secretary of State for Social Security using the word 'bogus' repeatedly, unsupported by any evidence.[204]

The independent Glidewell Inquiry panel heard submissions from community workers who testified that children in playgrounds were referring to refugees as 'bogus', 'scroungers', 'beggars', 'dirty' and 'disgusting'.[205]

Former Shadow Home Secretary Gerald Kaufman has commented that even in parliament, debates tend to take place as if ethnic minorities are a breed apart. Reacting to the 1995 Bill he said:

> I fear that by participating in the debate at all I too am joining in the worst discrimination of all. Millions of our fellow citizens are being discussed as though they cannot hear. Our Asian and black constituents are being talked about as potential invaders of our country, and as potential bogus applicants for social security benefit and for housing benefit. They are being talked about as though they cannot hear what we are saying and as separate, different and inferior.[206]

In 1996, the United Nations Committee on the Elimination of Racial Discrimination concluded that xenophobia and racism were at unacceptably high levels in the UK, a situation which it attributed, in part, to the way in which negative images of refugees and asylum seekers had been promoted by some politicians and some sections of the media.[207]

Dr Craig Young analysed the Ministerial statements and speeches used to justify the Immigration and Asylum Bill of 1995. He concluded that the Government had, in the most part, sold the Bill to create the impression of strong government and had, as further justification, used the underlying theme that democracy and freedom were at risk without such measures. Asylum seekers had been presented overwhelmingly as a threat. Part of the context which had also been successfully exploited was the national self-image of Britain as a country with a good record on providing asylum. This 'package' worked and did influence public opinion even if some of the information was selective, incomplete, even untenable, says Dr Young:

> In these constructions it is the irresponsibility of those individuals who are prepared to abuse the system and of those who are prepared to profit by employing illegal immigrants which is to blame for the increase in applications, not geopolitical reality.[208]

A study by Ronald Kaye published in 1996 concluded that there was insufficient evidence to show that the media had set the agenda on public attitudes to asylum seekers adding: ' On the contrary, we would argue that, on our evidence, concerns of the public are more likely to be shaped by political elites, with the media playing a largely intermediary role.'[209]

The images handed down from 1962, of 'tides' 'floods' and 'swamps' were re-used with some success. The central message echoed by Home Secretary Michael Howard was that Britain should be 'a haven not a honeypot.'[210] When he announced in 1995 the new measures to stop perceived abuse of the social security system by temporary visitors, he portrayed those people as out to 'milk the system for all they can get.'[211] Such language opened the door to a Conservative MP, Winston Churchill, to say in 1993 that immigrants were 'flocking to this country in banana boats.' and that there were 'more and more hungry mouths and bellies coming here in search of the good life.' Some people are so persuaded that illegal immigrants are the enemy within that they think they have a right to react with hostility. This must explain why the repeated desecration of the grave of Joy Gardener, the black mother who died in front of her four year old son after being bound and gagged by police trying to deport her.[212]

The Glasgow Media Group has produced further evidence that the way in which the issue of immigration, communicated to the public via the media, has contributed to creating fear and hostility and prevented a rational discussion of immigration.[213]

For this project, IPPR asked the Home Office for all of its press releases relating to ethnic minorities over a period of two years, 1994-1996. The pack sent to us contained 24 press releases. All were concerned with immigration:

- 12 were on illegal immigrants and 'bogus' refugees and measures to deal with these problems

- 5 announced visa restrictions for various countries, all non-white except for Peru

- 1 was information on the work of the immigration and nationality department

- 4 were on technical changes to travel documents and forms

- 1 provided information on the 1995 Immigration and Asylum Act

- 1 was a positive initiative to assist Bosnian refugees.

Comments in the press releases attributed to Ministers covered three areas:

- That good race relations depended on tight immigration policies

- The problem of illegal immigrants and 'bogus' refugees and the necessity for vigilance and regulation

- The cost to the taxpayer of these migrants living off the state or working illegally.

The words 'bogus', 'racketeers', 'abuse', and 'fraudsters' appear with frequency as did emotive statements about asylum seekers 'milking the system' and the British tax payer having to shoulder burdens.

Only two positive statements appear to have been made:

- In October 1995, Home Secretary Michael Howard spoke about the need to help Bosnian refugees settle in this country. Three million pounds were made available to create a helpline to provide assistance to 500 Bosnian refugees and to provide other schemes to enable the refugees to overcome their difficulties. Howard said: 'These Bosnian families are in desperate need of help. We were the first EU country to respond to a call from the UNHCR to help those caught up in the conflict. The help we are offering will provide much needed refuge for these people.'[214]

- In July 1996 Minister Timothy Kirkhope spoke of the contributions made by immigrants and refugees. At the end of a long statement on the threat of 'bogus' asylum seekers and illegal immigrants, Kirkhope said: 'Those who have sought refuge or settlement have made a vital contribution and I am sure will continue to do so.'

One of the most striking examples of a Home Office press release which had the potential to affect adversely both white and black public opinion was one which announced the use of sniffer dogs to find illegal immigrants. It contained thirteen points on the welfare and well being of the dogs, including information on what they were fed, and enthusiastically pointed out that 'Billy found some illegals on his first training session at Dover'.[215] The tone and content elevated the lives of the dogs above those of the 'illegals'. Race advisors at the Home Office confirmed that they had not been consulted for comment on the tone of this or many of the other press releases. When questioned on this, a senior Home Office official said that such press releases were often sent out to 'win over papers like the *Daily Mail* and *The Express*. They show them that we are tough and dependable on this issue.'

There has been a remarkable shift in presentation since the election. Forty press releases were made available to the IPPR by October 1998. Seven of them dealt with abusers of the immigration rules and asylum regulations. Words like 'abusive' and 'illegals' were found in these as were claims that many of these people were guilty of 'blatant deceit.' The rest of the press releases, even those dealing with controversial policies, provided facts and figures without rhetoric and ten of them concentrated on positive attributes of immigrants and multicultural Britain.

The Media

An unresolved issue is whether the media creates or reflects public opinion. In his well researched booklet on the popular press and the 1992 election, Martin Linton makes a convincing case for the former. For newspapers in particular to claim that they make no difference is untenable says Linton:

> All newspaper advertising and therefore the newspaper industry itself is built on the premise that newspapers can influence the behaviour of their readers. To argue that newspapers cannot influence their reader's voting decisions but can influence their purchasing decisions is irrational.[216]

David McKie of *The Guardian* makes a similar point:

> To claim to have no influence over the decisions opinions and attitudes of readers would be a suicide note sent to all advertisers.[217]

Having established his case that papers can influence attitudes, Linton shows convincingly that the most astute politicians we have had in recent years – including Harold Wilson and Margaret Thatcher – knew how to use the papers. They had a direct relationship with the press owners, editors and key journalists. Wilson and Thatcher were particularly keen to establish a bond with *The Sun* and they did. The paper in turn supported them and made a difference to the election results in the case of Thatcher and helped Wilson sell some difficult policies to the nation. Blair has a similar 'active' relationship with the popular press and the support he obtained during the election reflects that relationship. Co-operation is already happening on a number of issues. Our contention is that, in relation to race relations, more could be done to enable new messages to be put out without Labour being hounded in old predictable ways.

Correcting misinformation

The Home Office, during the previous government's term of office, was unable to tell the IPPR how often misinformation in the media was corrected by the press office, or by what mechanisms. From newspaper cuttings, however, it is clear that when Charles Wardle resigned as the Immigration Minister in July 1994, claiming that the government policies on immigration and Europe would 'flood' this country with millions of immigrants and immigrant workers, the Home Office did respond to some of the media coverage. Wardle's claims were challenged. The 'millions' of foreigners whom he claimed could come to work in the UK included EU citizens and British black and Asian people and this was made clear by government sources.[218]

Briefing journalists

The formal relationships between the media and the government are clear. Information is circulated through press releases and briefings. As important are the informal networks, the off-the-record conversations which are not easily scrutinised, not least because both sides disclaim such a 'live' relationship. Discussions with staff in the Home Office, the Immigration Service and with 16 journalists confirmed that informal communication does of course take place.

Speaking to the annual conference of the Refugee Legal Centre on 19 November 1997, Immigration Minister Mike O'Brien acknowledged that:

> Officials may in the past have fed stories to tabloid journalists. We have made it clear that we do not want them to do so. Some may nevertheless talk unofficially and I can't give you a guarantee that it won't happen.

The Immigration Service Union, (ISU) wishing to highlight the importance of a well resourced immigration service, are known to have passed information about 'illegal' immigrants to newspapers and journalists with known anti-immigration views.[219] The union openly agreed with Charles Wardle's claims about the dangers of millions of people coming to settle.[220] Correspondence from the ISU to two Home Secretaries between 1992 and 1993 leaked to the IPPR suggests that the ISU actively encouraged hard line policies on asylum seekers. Politicians have also intervened directly to influence the media. In a highly publicised case in December 1995, a Conservative Party worker directly offered a journalist 'background' information on an applicant seeking asylum in order to undermine his claim. The journalist was told by the party worker that this was being done 'because we do not feel we have got our case across on this one.'[221] In another case Home Office Minister Timothy Kirkhope reprimanded *The Evening Standard* for supporting an applicant and adverse publicity was at the same time leaked by the Immigration and Nationality Department to *The Sunday Express*.[222]

These examples illustrate that in relation to immigration, there has been in the past no clear line between the demands of party politics, trade union politics and the importance of disseminating accurate policy information. Government ministers and officials have the right to use the available channels to brief journalists and inform the public about immigration policies, facts and figures, but it is appropriate to ask whether the way that has been done in the past contributed to public anxiety. Given the ease with which government could secure coverage in negative stories it is pertinent to ask why stories and information have not been placed which might help redress the balance of coverage.

Shifting position

Towards the end of the period of Conservative government, there were signs of recognition that the damage caused by the immigration debate had to be addressed. In a memo to the then Home Secretary, Michael Howard, leaked to *The Guardian* in 1995, Employment Minister Gillian Shepherd expressed her worries that the 1996 Asylum Bill would encourage racial discrimination.[223] In November, of the same year, John Major, then Prime Minister, was sufficiently worried that racial tensions would be inflamed by the Asylum Bill to consider setting up a Standing Committee, a suggestion from Tony Blair who wanted to re-establish consensus on race and immigration 'so it wasn't a thing of party politics'.

Some of this caution extended to the 1997 election campaign. In spite of efforts by some in the Conservative party to raise immigration, their views were marginal to the campaign. An unprecedented agreement had been reached when the parties, encouraged by the

Commission for Racial Equality, signed a pledge saying that a balance would be struck between the principles of free speech and the responsibility of politicians not to stir up 'hostility between people of different racial or national groups.'[224] The party leaders not only showed restraint in refusing to use the race card, but also made pre-election speeches on the benefits that immigrants have brought to this country. Feelings were aroused among black and Asian Britons when the Labour party used the bulldog symbol to promote the idea of patriotism. However, compared with the populist anti-immigrant sentiments that swept through many previous elections, these were minor blemishes on an unusually clean and positive campaign.

IPPR carried out a straw poll in April 1997 of fifty people from ethnic communities to find out whether they thought public attitudes towards minorities were influenced by politicians prior to the election.[225] Equally divided between men and women, they included a cross section of people from the various communities. Of those prepared to disclose their political allegiances, twenty turned out to be Labour supporters; six supported the Liberal Democrats and three the Conservatives. Twelve were between the ages of 19 and 24. They all held, or had held, positions of influence in their communities and/or in their professions. The private, charitable and voluntary sectors were all represented and the interviews were done either privately or with small groups under conditions of confidentiality.

- The majority of the interviewees felt that, on the whole, the three leaders were projecting the right, positive messages on multiculturalism through the speeches they were making.

- Most of the interviewees felt that there had been an important shift in the Conservative party after John Major took over. In contrast to Margaret Thatcher, whom they felt was threatened by multiculturalism, Major was seen as someone who was at ease with it and more able therefore to change attitudes in the party and the country. As one teacher put it: 'He grew up in Brixton. He knows us. He has also come from nowhere so he understands struggle.'

- More than twenty interviewees felt that Labour was still the best party for black and Asian voters but even in this group, several commented that the party was too afraid of middle England and the possible revival of its reputation as 'politically correct' and 'loony' to be seen to be taking and interest in black and Asian Britons. The comparison was made between Labour's stand on women and on ethnic minorities, and at least half the Labour voters said that this invisibility was giving the wrong message to the rest of the British public about black and Asian Britons.

● All bar one of the interviewees said the Labour party's use of the bulldog and past images of Britain and patriotism were offensive, especially as the bulldog is used by extremist nationalist organisations as their symbol. They knew that Labour was attempting to reclaim the symbols of patriotism but were not convinced that this was the way to do it. Concern was expressed at the message this was giving to white and non-white Britons.[226]

Since the election of the Labour government, there have been positive signs that Ministers take the issues of language and presentation seriously. The Home Office team, in informal talks with the Black Jewish Forum (a network of black, Asian and Jewish individuals) has for instance discussed the use of less emotive and more accurate words for those asylum seekers whose applications are rejected because they do not meet the criteria. It was suggested by the Black Jewish Forum that 'ineligible' might be a better alternative and at a meeting in March 1998, Jack Straw and Mike O' Brien informed the BJF that they now no longer used the prefix 'bogus' for failed asylum seekers.[227] In November 1998 Mike O'Brien publicly stated that the word 'bogus' would no longer be used by the government when describing asylum seekers without a case. It was suggested however that 'abusive' should be used instead. The impact of this is unlikely to be any less damaging. [228]

Positive contribution

One development in recent times has been the acknowledgement, finally, of the contributions made by ethnic minorities to this country. Key people in politics have begun to acknowledge publicly the sacrifices made by thousands of black and Asian people who gave their lives in the two World Wars, the central role they played in the creation of the National Health Service, British Rail and London Transport, and how their small businesses have transformed urban areas.

Lord McIntosh of Haringey, opposing the 1995 Asylum and Immigration Bill:

> [The Bill] is full of poison. It is full of unjustified and ill-conceived prejudice against many people who come to the country and enrich our lives. They have done so for 1000, 2000 and probably more years. Our lifeblood in this country has been immigration.'[229]

Positive speeches are an important indicator of how the culture of politics may be changing across the board. Even within the right wing of the Conservative party, there is evidence that their view of the nation is becoming more inclusive. At a conference organised by the CRE, when talking about discrimination, prejudice and violence, Michael Howard, then Home Secretary, said the issues:

> go to the heart of the quality of life not only of the three million people in Britain who are members of the ethnic minorities, but the whole of the population. For the quality of life of every citizen is enhanced if we live in harmony with one another; it is diminished if we live in discord.[230]

Tony Blair, then leader of the Opposition, speaking at the opening of an Anne Frank exhibition, said on the subjects of racism and anti-Semitism:

> They are evils which eat at the heart of too many of our communities today and we should not rest until they are eradicated. My vision is of a Britain which is genuinely 'one nation' where shared values of social justice, tolerance of difference and liberty from oppression unite us all. I am passionately committed to creating a society where every individual, regardless of colour, creed or race is afforded the same opportunity and respect for his or her neighbour. That means a society where Jews, Muslims, Hindus and Christians are free to worship, where our expectations of black and Asian children are high and where no-one fears attack for reason of the colour of their skin or background.[231]

He spoke of multiculturalism as an enriching and positive feature of this country. The issue here these days is not that these sentiments are not expressed enough, but that they are almost always delivered to the converted like anti-racist or black and Asian organisations. This is as true of New Labour as it was for the Conservative government judging by the many excellent, positive speeches made by Jack Straw and Mike O'Brien in the first 19 months of office copies of which were made available to the IPPR.

When John Major visited India as Prime Minister he made memorable, positive statements about the ethnic communities in Britain. That speech, because it was so unequivocal, was widely commented on. He spoke of the fact that there had been a doubling of trade between the two countries since his last visit there in 1993, and now stood at £3.5 billion. This fact alone could have a significant impact on the British image of Indians. Many Britons still perceive India to be full of people seeking aid rather than as a big players in our domestic economy.[232]

Tony Blair, when Leader of the Opposition, made a similarly powerful speech at a gathering organised by prominent Asians. Speaking at the 25th anniversary celebration of the Gujarat Samachar, an Asian newspaper, he spoke of the achievements of the community, how much Asians had contributed to British life and how he felt the majority population could learn something about responsibility and family life from British Asians.[233]

At events organised by the ethnic communities, Michael Howard, when Home Secretary, made speeches which again were appreciative. At the Sikh celebration to celebrate the birth of one of their Gurus in July 1995, he said:

> I am very pleased to see that today's events include honouring those who fought with us in the Second World War. Their courage, their sacrifices and their dedication should never be forgotten.[234]

while in August 1995, at the opening of the Neasdon temple, he said

> The Hindu Community has made a committed contribution to the life of this country and has enriched it in many ways.

We welcome diversity and the richness which other cultures
bring to the fabric of our society. This Mandir is evidence of
that richness and diversity.[235]

Addressing black and Asian Britons in this way is important. It helps the
communities to have their presence and attainments proclaimed. But if
these are the only occasions that such speeches are made, their impact
is limited and the motivation increasingly becomes so suspect that even
the minorities are not convinced by their authenticity. Opportunities to
spread that message have been wasted. If the majority population were
regularly exposed to the positive sentiments that have been expressed to
minorities, their attitudes could be influenced.

There are, however, signs that political leaders are beginning to give
these messages to influential white people. In May 1998 Tony Blair
spoke to some of Britain's top business leaders at a CRE conference on
leadership and race equality:

There is an obligation and duty upon all of us who are in
positions of leadership within the community to try and offer
a lead to everyone else. I may say that includes the
Government itself and all the political parties... What is
involved here is not just some symbol or signal of goodwill. It
is a genuine test to send a message right across British society
that we regard living in a multicultural, multiracial country as
a positive plus for this country. Not something that we need
to be worried or concerned about, but something that we go
out and celebrate and say our country is better as a result of
having that type of society around us.[236]

Inconsistent message

For black and Asian Britons, assurances that their contribution is valued
are undermined by the reality of immigration decisions affecting their
families. The discretionary powers of immigration officers to exclude
visitors regularly mean that old parents have not been allowed to visit
their families and there are ghostly absences at wedding feasts and even
more poignant ones at funerals.[237] Families are kept apart and this does
not persuade ethnic minorities that they are valued and equal citizens.

Positive speeches about contributions then sound unconvincing. Roy Hattersley, referring to words spoken by John Major at the Commonwealth Institute[238] about the 'important, thoughtful, and highly appreciated' contribution made by Asians to the country, pointed out the injustice suffered by an elderly Sikh man who was refused leave to visit his family in this country for what appeared to be utterly spurious reasons:

> His son and the other Sikhs who came to see me are insulted by the irrationality of so arbitrary a decision. They believe that the reason the old man's application was turned down was because he was from the Indian subcontinent. And they are right. Had he been an Australian, Canadian or New Zealander, he would, even now, be enjoying his son's company. So much for 'highly respected contribution'.[239] So great is the need now to belong, and so anxious are ethnic minorities not to be identified with the problem paradigm associated with immigration, that many are expressing sympathy with tight immigration laws. They fear that more will mean even less for them. It is not an endorsement of existing immigration policies, but an indicator of how insecure many black and Asians feel in this country. In IPPR's survey of attitudes, more Asians than whites believed that there was too much immigration to this country. In the same study, Asians were found to be the prime targets of racial prejudice. Interestingly, the majority of all groups interviewed did not believe that prejudice would decline if all immigration were banned.[240]

Myths and misinformation

Immigration is often discussed without facts and figures. Often these are simply not available, sometimes it is because they remain unpublicised. The complexity of what is happening is rarely understood by the public. As Anne Singleton, an academic expert on immigration statistics, says: 'the complexity of migration patterns and processes is rarely communicated to the public'.[241]

Although the popular press reports obsessively on those who are thought to be cheating the immigration authorities or the benefits agencies, there has been a striking dearth of information on the real situation of those legitimately seeking asylum and the subsequent outcome or on their mistreatment by officials in this country. Anne Applebaum, writing in *The Spectator*[242] during the debate on the 1995 Bill:

> While voters have become aware of the ways in which politicians can manipulate budgets and inflation rates to produce feel-good factors of one sort and other, they are less likely to question the bogusness of rhetoric about bogus asylum seekers and illegal immigrants. Invariably the arguments against foreigners are economic; they are stealing from the state, taking jobs from the British ... but is that image fair?

By working as nannies and cleaners, they enable thousands of British women to go to work. By working in restaurants, they help recycle money from the rich into the rest of the economy. By working in the building sites, they contribute to the value of housing stock. And by buying things – hi-fi equipment, television sets, video recorders ... they boost high street spending figures. However squarely political critics aim their fire at bogus asylum seekers, the economic arguments which are deployed against immigrants don't hold up ... there isn't enough evidence that they damage the economy.

As human beings, black and Asian Britons, as well as refugees and asylum seekers have their share of criminals, dropouts and failures. This needs to be pointed out by government officials when the media unfairly links undesirable activities with race or immigration status. In November 1998, the *Daily Mail* had a front page story claiming that large numbers of asylum seekers were engaged in serious crime. The damage done by such stories is incalculable and it is the responsibility of the government to inject balance and facts into such biased reports. Ministers these days often get space in newspapers to write their own views. Very few have chosen to tackle these issues in their columns.

Conclusion

This historical account reveals how the terms of the debate on immigration, race relations and integration in Britain were laid down. Immigration policies have been justified as necessary to race relations with no demonstrable benefits to either area. The damaging effects of contradictory messages about immigrants and about black and Asian Britons have rarely been considered. Mixed messages have been given out by politicians and the tendency has been to follow public prejudice rather than lead, change and inform public opinion. Insufficient attention has been given to the need for coherent integration policies which would influence public attitudes and educate the population – black and white – on the realities of multicultural Britain and the changes that have taken place in the demographics, cultural and political life of this country. Myths have settled and rarely been challenged until politicians began, in recent years, to inject some balance into the debate by drawing attention to the positive contribution which immigrants, refugees and members of minority communities have made. There is also a tendency to speak too little of the rights of ethnic communities, asylum seekers and refugees. No community should be expected to hold up its achievements constantly as a condition of their presence here. Unsurprisingly therefore, fifty years after Windrush, indigenous Britons are still ignorant about and prejudiced against their black and Asian compatriots.

4. A new strategy

This chapter sets out the arguments for government to lead public opinion towards an inclusive perception of nationhood, multiculturalism and the role of minority communities within that vision. It advocates a new strategy, draws on some positive lessons from abroad and suggests in practical terms how that strategy could be implemented.

Redefining Britain, multiculturalism and the nation: the goal

For too long the term multiculturalism has referred only to non-white Britons, not to society as a whole. The British nation has been regarded by many as white with multiculturalism existing only at the margins. The project to redefine these terms has begun with the Prime Minister himself who increasingly is giving a new inclusive description of the British identity. Our argument is that the Government should go further, embarking on a well planned project to redefine multicultural Britain as an inclusive concept which embraces diversity and values the contribution of all its members. Bill Clinton initiated such an integrated strategy for the United States in 1996. The interim report produced on this initiative asserted the need for such a transforming strategy and stated that such a project needed to be given time, commitment from the top and resources.[243] It also shows how the impact of such an ambitious project needs to be led by the most powerful political person in the country.

The perception that multicultural policies only concern non-whites needs to be challenged because this view has caused problems and this is particularly true of education policies. Education researcher Roger Hewitt describes the negative effect of many of these initiatives in a recent book based on primary research among white people in Greenwich, the area where the British National party has a stronghold and where three young black men, including Stephen Lawrence have been killed in racist attacks in recent years. Hewitt says of older models of multicultural education:

> white pupils seem like cultural ghosts, haunting as mere absences the richly decorated corridors of multicultural society.[244]

There is now a need for ethnic and religious pride to be encouraged in all the communities of Britain. This includes the English, Scottish, Welsh and Irish as well as all of the minority groups. The development of shared values and a core culture are essential and the recent debates about including education on citizenship values is a step in that direction. South Africa embarked on this project at the same time as the country was working out a new constitution. And as we approach the next century, it is time for the British government to rethink how a complex, mature, multiracial democracy should be governed, managed and progressed in the next century. The sense of purpose and destiny that politicians are attempting to create as we enter the next century will need, at least in part, to be constructed around the revaluation of multiculturalism and the benefits it brings. In the future we will have to become 'globally civilized' which means gaining confidence in dealing with diversity abroad. This will be impossible unless steps have been taken to make the British population comfortable with diversity within its own shores.

Before looking at the practical means government might use to get its message across it is useful to look at the strategies which have been used abroad in three countries which have made a deliberate attempt to address public opinion in this area.

Canada

Canada is a young country with considerable resources and problems of under-population in some areas. It sees and projects itself as a country of immigration where everyone, except the Native Canadians, are immigrants. Nevertheless, the country has started to face the kinds of problems and issues that are commonplace in Britain. A report in 1994 claimed:

> There has been a dramatic increase in incidents of racism and anti-Semitism over the past four years. Recorded incidents include the desecration of synagogues and graveyards, widespread racist graffiti and leafleting in high schools, college and university campuses, direct and brutal physical attacks, street riots ... [245]

Evidence has emerged in recent years of overt discrimination against some communities.[246] White Canadian residents are showing greater tendencies of xenophobia towards certain groups of immigrants, refugees and asylum seekers. There is now a tendency to describe old time immigrants as the 'real' Canadians and to see later arrivals as a threat to the earlier settlers. There is also a hierarchy forming in the minds of white Canadians that there are worthy and desirable immigrants, and immigrants and refugees of the undesirable sort. The Canadian social commentator, Margaret Cannon describes this vividly in her authoritative account of racism in Canada:

> We are, whether we like it or not, tribal by nature. We cling to our own kinds, our own ways, our own people. 'They' – the Other, be it Jews or Chinese or Blacks – are encroaching on 'our' privileges and place. White British Colombians complain that Chinese students are 'taking over' the University of British Colombia keeping 'our' kids out. In Ontario there are complaints about too many Orientals in the medial and pharmacy schools. Thirty years ago there were the same complaints about Jews.[247]

In British Colombia the arrival of new immigrants from Hong Kong during the past decade has created serious tensions because of fears that the area would become predominantly Chinese and because many were wealthy enough to buy properties at high prices.[248]

The officials to whom the author spoke in the Multicultural and Citizenship Department and in the Immigration Department were concerned that the multicultural programmes were now regarded by some white Canadians as a waste of public money. Questions were being asked about the need for immigration which was seen by some as bringing 'cultural problems';[249] and sections of the press were creating antipathy among the white population by running negative stories which focused on issues like forced marriages, the ethnic origins of criminals, and refugees and asylum claimants 'living off the state.'

It was also becoming clear that public opinion was volatile. In 1972 when stateless Ugandan Asians arrived in their thousands, public opinion in Canada had been overwhelmingly positive. The government and the people had worked together to receive and settle those refugees.

In 1986 when a boatload of Sri Lankans arrived seeking refuge, they were also almost universally welcomed by the Canadian population. Just a year later, when a boatload of Sikhs arrived in Nova Scotia, public opinion had become more suspicious and antagonistic. In the months in between, right wing politicians and the media had spoken out against the 'generosity' of Canada and begun to suggest that many of the asylum seekers were making false claims.[250]

Nevertheless, there remained a political consensus on most of the key issues in relation to race and immigration. Most national politicians refrained from using vociferous anti-immigration rhetoric. Only a minority was using race and immigration in order to appeal to the most xenophobic of Canadians.

National Government Strategies

The Canadian Government publicly acknowledges responsibility for influencing the wider population on immigration and multiculturalism. In the 1992/93 Annual Report on the operation of the Canadian Multicultural Act, Sheila Finestone wrote:

> The Multicultural Programme is a key instrument that promotes the diversity that is our reality today and underscores the fact that pluralism is the hallmark of Canadian society... The Government of Canada has an important and demanding role to play in the movement towards building a better country. It is a challenge we accept without reservation. We are committed to demonstrating leadership to ensure that all departments and agencies understand the benefits of diversity in our society ... much more remains to be done to demonstrate that our policy is inclusive of all Canadians.[251]

The policies in Canada to develop positive attitudes towards minority groups are based on an underpinning ideal which is stated and restated by Ministers across departments. This is that Canada is a country of immigration where diversity is valued but where there are core principles which bind all Canadians. An integrated strategy has been developed to promote these ideals. This includes transparency about immigration and integration, meaningful public consultation, the collection and dissemination of accurate information and the facilitation of a culture of participation.

Promotion of ideals

In Canada the objectives of an integration policy were first set down in 1971 when the first multicultural policies were instituted. The vision then was based on a mosaic view of society and the emphasis placed by Prime Minister Pierre Trudeau was on the elimination of societal and institutional barriers to the participation and progress of ethnic minorities, the support of their own cultures and the sharing of their values with other Canadians. These ideals were then turned into three policy objectives: to promote 'other group' acceptance, cultural heritage and inter-group sharing and contact. A number of programmes were set up, or funded, to achieve these goals.

By the Nineties the process remains the same but the goals have changed. In order to prevent fragmentation and promote the idea of a nation which is diverse but bonded, the heritage budget which was used to promote in-group cultures has been halved, but the race relations and community participation budget, which includes public education and cross cultural understanding, has been substantially increased.

In 1998 a new programme mandate was announced by the Department of Multiculturalism:

> Strengthening Canada by fostering an inclusive society in which people of all backgrounds, whose identities are respected and recognised as vital to an evolving Canadian identity, feel a sense of belonging and attachment to this country.[251]

Canadians are constantly reminded in different ways that multiculturalism is an essential part of their national identity. All government Ministers make it a point to refer to the value of a multicultural Canada in their public speeches. In the two weeks of 16 November and 1 December 1 1995 which the author monitored, twelve speeches made by Ministers in the ruling Liberal Party Government from different departments referred to this issue and in positive terms. They stressed the humanitarian traditions of Canada, made pro-immigration arguments and described the benefits of diversity.

Since 1989 a day has been set aside (21 March) as the International day for the Elimination of Racial Discrimination. The reason given for instituting such a day was that: 'Raising public awareness of the nature, scope and impact of discrimination in our society is a necessary step towards eliminating it.'[253] Ministers attend events and make speeches.

High profile politicians attend the August Caribbean carnival and other such celebrations and the events are described as essentially and positively Canadian. A whole week is set aside to promote the concept of citizenship, rights and responsibilities. Central to this are public education activities which reinforce the Canadian Charter of Rights and Freedoms. This is reassuring for those who feel that their core values might be eroded by ethnic groups pushing for cultural autonomy and it is also important for recent immigrants who need to understand the enormous importance and implications of the Charter.

Canada, like South Africa, has also evolved the meaning of the word multiculturalism to include everyone. Weiner describes the Multicultural Act as something for:

> Black Canadians, white Canadians, Canadians of every colour and origin possible; Canadians by choice and by birth, Canadians who are Christians, Jews, Muslims, Hindus, and members of every other faith ... people from every calling and every ceiling. [254]

This is illuminating and does call into question the way multiculturalism has been interpreted in Britain. Was it, for example, wise always to describe integration in terms of discrimination and exclusion? Would it have been more effective if more inclusive visions had been put forward which went beyond discrimination?

The rights and responsibilities model is also carefully worked out in Canada. Much emphasis is placed on the symbolism and meaning of citizenship. In order to obtain citizenship, applicants are expected to learn about the principles of multiculturalism and what is expected of Canadian citizens. Teaching material is made available across Canada and those who eventually do go through the process appear to believe that they have joined something of profound significance. The citizenship ceremonies are solemn and again intended to draw an emotional response from those achieving that privilege. At these ceremonies, which take place in local areas as well as in government buildings in city centres, Ministers often attend, drawing media attention. The aim is to reinforce the commonality of citizenship to balance the value of diversity.

There is a Canadian citizenship week when various festivals are held and where there is a national affirmation of pride in citizenship. On Canada Day, selected new citizens are honoured. Citations are made to individuals who have been felt to contribute to race relations. The Charter of Rights and Freedoms and the Constitution reinforce these positive messages and are in turn reinforced by many of these rituals.

There is a wide assumption that immigrants and refugees who have 'made good' must pass on their success and 'pay back' by sponsoring a refugee or befriending them. Tax benefits are made available. Some of these initiatives fail, others do better. When they do work, publicity ensures that Canadians become aware that refugees do not remain dependants forever. Some Ugandan Asians have recently sponsored refugees from embattled areas of the ex-Soviet Union and Afghanistan and the public takes great pride in such developments.

Besides the human rights and values message, officials and politicians have been emphasising the benefits of multiculturalism to business. Information is given out to the public on how the Canadian Grain Commission has employed immigrants with knowledge and languages of non-European countries to secure international trade. People are told how, for example, trade missions to Hong Kong and Taiwan took Chinese Canadians and helped to welcome business people from the Far East and Japan into Canada, and how the Asia Pacific Foundation facilitates business and tourism and is one of the most successful partnerships in existence. Such facts are frequently presented by Ministers and in government press releases.

Public awareness kits on the advantages and implications of diversity in Canada have been distributed to the provinces. Facts are provided to illustrate the historical importance of immigration to the country, to show that immigration is being properly managed, to dispel myths about special treatment, and to sensitise people about the problems faced by newcomers. These are active and participatory. Much of the material is drawn out of public consultation exercises and a serious attempt is made to deal with each major anxiety that has been expressed.

Officials endeavour to ensure that messages are responsive to the public mood. Where once Canadians might have been worried that they were becoming isolationist, and therefore respond to campaigns which promoted internationalism, now they are much less likely, according to research evidence, to feel as strongly about that issue as they are about diversity within Canada. The content of the message, the timing and context is obviously very important.

Campaigns are also evaluated. In 1993 for example, the Multicultural and Citizenship department carried out focus group research to gather evidence of public responses to some of their education campaigns on racism. Subsequent materials reflected what they had learnt.[255]

Each year, the Immigration Minister sets out the rational for current immigration and plans for the coming year. In the report for 1994, the then Minister Sergio Marchi said:

> Immigration policy represents one of the most important and complex challenges facing Canada today. It is, perhaps more than any other area of public policy, tied to our history – to the development of our values, our cultural diversity, the regional and economic dynamics of our nation. It will, in the long run, help to determine the character of our country in the years ahead... Our goal is to benefit Canada, to benefit Canadians, and to benefit everyone who had faith in the enormous potential of our country... I am open to an open and progressive immigration policy ... but I am also committed to a realistic immigration policy.[256]

Later in the statement the Minister said that Canada would be a much less vibrant country without immigrants and that decisions on immigration would determine the future for the children of Canada.

Other innovative initiatives are being used to influence perceptions. A well researched television drama with high production values, *Land of Hope*, was financed in 1995 by the Citizenship and Immigration Department. This had interwoven, emotionally-charged stories of seven families who had settled in Canada. The aim was to help people to understand and identify with immigrants in a way that was entertaining and engaging. A video of the lives and achievements of Ugandan Asians was widely distributed. A ceremony in Ottawa attended by the Prime Minister celebrated the achievements of those who arrived penniless and, for many, in a terrible emotional state. Canadians feel immense pride about this particular success story. In other videos which have been produced and disseminated across the country one of the central themes is that of historical continuity from the enormous sacrifices of Chinese and Sikh workers who built the railways to the present time.

Most importantly, the concept of multiculturalism is always inclusive of white Canadians and their own historical contributions. The thrust is therefore not of special treatment but of a national project. This is something that needs to be considered in Britain, where for far too long the concept has been used to describe non-white Britons.[257]

That spirit is present in much of the publicity material produced by the various government departments. For example, posters challenging stereotypes and self perceptions are regularly used around metropolitan areas. Some are deliberately provocative; most are inclusive and they feature the faces of white and non white Canadians. One range of such posters says for instance: 'They are all the same. Are they? Are you?'

Research

Statistics on immigrants are collected and published regularly. Figures are not, however, only gathered on the numbers of people entering the country; a tracking process then records what is happening to a cross-section of them and how they are faring.

The fact that attitudes towards immigration have been studied in Canada since 1945 means that progress, abrupt changes and correlations with external factors like developments in the labour market can be trailed and interpreted. The data gathered provides politicians with empirical material to use in their speeches and in developing policy. Controversial facts can be dealt with honestly and with integrity.

Public opinion

Attitudes surveys are also used to test values and the information used for education campaigns. For example, research by the Economic Council indicated that Canadians value tolerance highly.[258] Messages which emphasised that quality rather than simply the facts of discrimination would therefore be more effective. The report also reached the conclusion, after a detailed literature review and their own research, that there was:

> little indication of a backlash or of an increase in prejudice as a result of the growing proportion of visible-minority immigrants in Canada ... we found evidence of increasing tolerance over time. There was also evidence that the proportion of visible-minority immigrants residing in the community was positively related to tolerance and to attitudes towards immigration.[259]

In 1991 a national survey was carried out by the federal government to provide 'public opinion information to be used for developing policy, public education and communication initiatives.'[260] Qualitative research was conducted using focus groups and a telephone survey was carried out in parallel.

Among the many areas explored were the following:

- Canadian values and identity

- support for multicultural policies

- limits to tolerance

- prejudice and discrimination

Some of the findings illustrate how developed the thinking is among Canadians on some of these issues, perhaps because theirs is a country where participation has been encouraged and where there is an ongoing discussion of national identity and national values. For example, when asked if they agreed with the statement 'The unity of this country is weakened by Canadians of different ethnic and cultural backgrounds sticking to their own ways' a third of the population disagreed, a third agreed and 16 per cent were neutral. When asked if the government's multicultural policy is 'vital to uniting Canada', 79 per cent believed this to be the case.

Meyer Burstein, then head of government immigration research, recognised the key part played by research in public education policy:

Research enables the government to give greater attention to educating the public by providing the facts. There is a consensus that research has improved the level of public debate.[261]

Public consultation

Canadian law requires the government to consult the public about immigration policy. Consultation exercises are carried out every three years and are intended to be a two way process between the government and the citizens of Canada. Opinions are gathered from over 10,000 people across the country. Specially trained people facilitate group discussions and there are discussion packs which are provided to groups who request it. The entire exercise operates at a local level.[262]

The basic idea here is not radical. It is no different from the People's Panel of 5000 which was set up to respond to Labour government policies and thinking on various issues. But on race and immigration, such consultations are simply not carried out in Britain.

The exercise in Canada is genuine and driven by Ministers. It is seen as a partnership between the people, provincial governments and the federal government. There has to be the right balance between the provision of facts and advocacy; between allowing extremist views while tapping into the largest group which hold middle of the road opinions. The skilful way in which elected representatives have not allowed themselves to become the prisoners of prejudiced public opinion, while allowing it to be ventilated, and have used informed opinion to find acceptable policies is something that would be invaluable here.

The Netherlands

The Netherlands is an interesting synthesis of the Canadian model of integration and the traditional British approach. Much of what the government is trying to do is similar to the vision more completely developed in Canada. As in Britain, however, public attitudes to immigration are far from positive and the linking of race relations to immigration has created barriers to truly innovative policies. Nevertheless a process of new thinking and developing good practice has begun.

There is assertive official recognition that the country is multiethnic and that it is the role of government to create a society 'in which the members of ethnic minorities, individually as well as collectively, have sound and equal opportunities and a social position that is equivalent to that of the indigenous Dutch.[263]

The model that is favoured is one where different groups have the right to maintain their cultures – the government funds denominational schools of many kinds – but that in exchange minorities should be aware that a number of the fundamental values of Dutch society are not negotiable. These include the democratic rule of the law, freedom of speech, the individuals' right to self determination, the equality of men and women and the separation of church and state.'[264]

The emphasis in the Netherlands is on the importance of the country living up to the principles of fundamental human rights. This is regarded as precious by leaders and citizens and is part of the self-esteem of the nation.

A detailed qualitative study published in 1995 demonstrated the need for government to take the lead in addressing attitudes. Based on strong theoretical concepts, it produced some persuasive evidence on the attitudes of indigenous Dutch people towards the minorities. It found that there was a variety of ways that racial prejudice was manifested and rationalised:[265]

- Beliefs in the biological or (more commonly) cultural superiority of the indigenous in-group and the tendency to think that the values of the majority group were the universal norm.

- An inclination to blame minority groups for bringing 'troubles' to the country.

- A tendency to generalise the negative characteristic of ethnic minority communities and individualise the achievements.

- Negative tolerance mechanisms which amounted to indigenous in-groups having no meaningful interactions with minority communities or making 'special' efforts to understand 'their' ways.

- A proclaimed neutrality which has come from a belief that there is no common humanity between different ethnic groups and that it is inevitable that ethnically different people lead separate lives.

● Paternalism based on feelings of cultural superiority.

● Forced anti-racism and resentment of pressure to conform to what is acceptable to say and do.

Devolution of responsibility

The one striking thing in the Netherlands – which among the European countries is most like Britain in terms of official thinking on race, ethnicity and discrimination – is the mutual respect and shared goals which exist between non-governmental organisations working in race relations and the government. It is through funding and supporting those organisations that much of the promotional work is carried out.

Information is deemed to be very important. The government funds information campaigns by interested parties and subsidises anti-racist consultation meetings between the churches, unions and other institutions meeting with various ethnic groups. At a local level, there is much innovative work supported by government. Part of the aim is to empower and 'emancipate' minorities and encourage their participation, and part of it is to alter the perceptions of the majority community. Government at local level has, for example, instigated group and neighbourhood discussions amongst different ethnic group living in the same area. The government also funds groups which are critical watchdogs of policies on race and integration.

Some of the most successful campaigns have been local ones based in areas where citizens have a shared sense of purpose and ideals. A paper delivered by official delegates of the Dutch government in Warsaw described inner city integration projects funded by the central government which encouraged different communities living in deprivation to 'exchange information and engage in joint activities. 'One method which was found to be popular was to help people living in the same apartment block to come together regularly and build personal relationships and understanding.[266]

It is through the mobilisation of shame and through reminders of the Second World War that some of the most effective messages have been delivered. The Queen's speeches refer to the role of minorities and a special tribute is always paid to the ethnic minority soldiers who fought with the allies in the Second World War. Ministers have spoken about the benefits of immigration, the Minister for Economic Development saying that the country needed new 'starters to keep the economy afloat.'[267]

Ministers have also organised rebuttals in the media. When government research in 1994 indicated that some minorities were disproportionately involved in drug dealing, a team of officials was set up to plan the strategy of communication before the material was released. Ministers across the board made it their business to come out and say that it was wrong to stereotype people and that ethnic minorities worked very hard to better their lives. Officials kept up the pressure on the media by providing alternative stories which received coverage. As a matter of policy Dutch Ministers refrain from making overtly negative statements about minority groups and do, when appropriate talk in terms of positive contributions. [268]

Germany

In many ways Germany is unique among the countries in the West because of its history. Germans have had to deal with defeat, economic collapse, massive national guilt, and the abhorrence that was unleashed towards the country and its people after the Second World War and the Holocaust. Rebuilding the nation and creating a non-threatening presence has preoccupied the country. Reunification provided another major challenge.

Attitudes and perceptions lag behind reality. Most Germans have only really understood racism in terms of the Holocaust. The self image of the country as a homogeneous homeland has persisted in spite of the fact that millions of non-indigenous people have lived and worked there since the end of the war. Here, perhaps more than most countries, one can see the complex relationship between history, migration, definitions of citizenship, and the changing notion of the nation-state. Germany has had problems managing integration because conceptually the country does not accept that it is a country of immigration. But unlike in Britain, this has led to a consensus of inaction. Not many people with power and influence see the need for an anti-discrimination policy nor even officially acknowledge the presence of a settled ethnic minority population. One German government official explained this:

We have so much to live down with the past. Most of us are
obsessed with the idea of 'never again'. We feel a terror when
we see any sign of anti-Semitism. But – and this is so strange
– we refuse to see racism against other groups. So our history
has made us guilty in some ways but the guilt and
responsibility stops there.[269]

Much has been written about German attitudes towards 'foreigners';
how even the language militates against any notion of a multiethnic
identity and equal rights for those who might have lived there for
generations. German nationality laws have been criticised because they
promote descent based definitions.[270] The presence and growth of neo-
Nazi groups and a fear that xenophobia could lead to terrible
consequences, all play their part in creating an image of a country that
has much to learn on anti-racism and where its people are often seen to
be intolerant. Economic uncertainties are exacerbating the situation.

Migrants in Germany, says David Nii Addy:

are increasingly perceived as illegitimate competitors an era of
structural change and more often than not used as handy
scapegoats.[271]

And yet, out of 80 million residents 8 per cent are foreigners and 60
per cent of them have lived there for more than ten years. 25 per cent
of all children born in Germany have one non-national parent. Millions
of migrants have entered Germany since the end of the war. Their
presence is almost always discussed as a 'problem' even though
research has demonstrated that the net gains from migrants outstrip the
costs borne by the country to accommodated their presence.[272] A few
influential politicians and ministers have used such information to
affect attitudes and to counteract the effect of other politicians who
have tried to use the race card when discussing the high rates of
unemployment in the country. In 1997, the German president, Roman
Herzog, said that the economic strength of the country came partly
from the work of migrants.[273] But despite such interventions and the
massive contributions of migrants, Germans have generally been
resentful because there has never been an integration programme and
because of a very particular notion Germans have of their homeland.

At the end of the 1980s, 50 per cent of Germans said foreigners should be sent back. In 1992 this issue was the one that most exercised West Germans.

The language of discourse is particular and some would say, detrimental to integration and positive change. As Dietrich Thrannhardt says:

> Germany is not alone in the tendency to attribute negative connotations to certain groups of immigrants, and in reflecting in the allocated labels a fluctuating interpretation of whom is considered desirable and undesirable.[274]

What is particular, however, is the stress on the foreign status of immigrant groups and their German born children. But because the issues of public attitude and hostility are so stark in this country, some of the positive initiatives that have been developed are noteworthy.

At the national level, although the right has been increasingly vocal in its hostility to migrants, German politicians have been strikingly forthcoming in their condemnation of racial violence. At the enormous candle-lit vigils organised by white Germans in the wake of arson attacks in Rostok and elsewhere and at the funerals of victims, German politicians, local and national, made personal appearances and moving statements, thus giving out a very powerful message.

For the best example of what can be achieved to influence attitudes by government, however, one would have to look at the way reunification was managed in Germany. As Graeme Atkinson observes:

> For the Christian Democratic party there was little hesitation from the outset and almost the entire German media was set in motion to bring it to fruition... There began a propaganda blitz, perhaps the biggest in recent German history, to push events with a haste ... in the direction of German unification.[275]

Appropriately enough, it is the city of Berlin – which was the symbol of a divided Germany and now of reunification – that has also become a beacon for the rest of the country in relation to the integration migrants. This has largely been through initiatives undertaken by the Berlin

Auslanderbeauftragte which was set up by the government in 1981, public education being one of its main functions. Its aim is to raise awareness among Germans and to change their vision of Germany as a mono-ethnic state. Public discussions are held regularly to discuss how the city can become more tolerant and international.

Emine Demirbuken, one of its officials said in 1993:

> The process of changing one's ideas and views on the German side is happening only very hesitantly. Yet in Berlin there are noticeable examples of a new perspective.[276]

The bureau owes this reputation to the skills and absolute commitment of one key politician, Barbara John, of the Christian Democratic Party who in 1996 had been doing the job for twelve years. Steve Vertovec:

> Most Berliners irrespective of their political persuasions acknowledge Frau John's position as testimony to her popularity (especially with ethnic minority organisations) and effectiveness in public relations, dealings with the police, overtures to local legislators and other responsibilities which go with the office.[277]

Interviewed for this project, Barbara Johns was convinced that politicians and the way they speak on an issue has a profound effect on the public:

> Nobody in government now would make negative comments about women, nobody dares to because that is not acceptable in the culture any more. We need the same sense of responsibility to be created about the minorities.

She is convinced that in her country the messages that would work are those that talk of equal treatment and not 'special rights':

The Holocaust is a useful reminder of what can happen, but in Germany it is also a barrier to broadening the way we think about racism. Too many people

> think that we have done a lot to break from our past and that the job is done.[278]

John argues that for too long across the European Union and in Germany, it is the extreme right wing which has set the pace and that it is time for others to take the lead. John and her colleagues are seeking not only to alter the perception of ethnic minorities, but to change the language away from expressions like 'foreigners', 'guestworkers' and 'here-living-non-Germans'. In the end it is a process of deconstructing and reconstructing the idea of what Germany was and now is.

Berlin is and has been cosmopolitan since the 1920s and the population is expanding rapidly. It is about to become the capital city. It has an enormous sense of its own destiny and mission for that reason. Berlin is all set to introduce and to develop advanced modes of managing cultural diversity. Globalisation has also changed Germany says the researcher Jochen Blachke, thereby allowing multiculturalism to 'connect with ideas of global cultural diversity ... supported by the international advertising industry.'[279]

The main thrust of Barbara John's campaign is to present change as modern internationalism. 'Berlin must show others the way,' she declares,

> We must show respect for tolerance and coexistence. We have already done this for centuries and it is why people like to come here. It is natural for us. But we have to consciously understand how important that is.[280]

Berlin's public education campaigns are not meant to preach but to raise debate. Posters are placed on the underground asking: 'What is German?' In the background there are hundreds of 'answers' to the question. They include images, stereotypes, black and white faces, German stars of all backgrounds. Rhymes, riddles, slang, are all used to provoke interest and begin the process of questioning received wisdom. Other posters ask 'What is true?' Then, in 1994 the public were asked a question on a poster – 'What comes tomorrow?' and asked to send in their own images, statements and visions. Thousands of responses came in and some were selected to make further posters. John claims that the response was terrific:

> Either they protested or they added more things. But they started to think. They might think, that is rubbish, we have

better things but it worked, it really worked.[281]

Beer mats with the same questions were distributed in bars to encourage 'ferocious discussion'.

This approach is interactive and challenging. It involves white Germans and does not tell them what they should do or think.

The Auslanderbeauftragte provides advice and publicity to a multicultural radio station and this is shifting perceptions among the young. Barbara John herself appears on this station each month to take calls and engage with the public in discussions. If there is one lesson to be learnt from the way Berlin is taking the lead in Germany, it is that one person with the right leadership qualities and visions can achieve changes that were once unimaginable.

Other initiatives have been tried with more limited effect. A national campaign, 'Make Friends with a Foreigner' – designed to encourage Germans to interact with ethnic minorities was regarded by many minority groups as patronising.[282] Moreover, as integration into German society is the real aim, the word 'foreigner' is unhelpful. This shows how important it is to get the message right. Cornelia Jacobson, John's counterpart in Bonn, feels that what is needed is more real and accurate information about the different groups who live in Germany:

> Most politicians are not as well informed as they need to be
> and that is why they make stereotypes.[283]

The message

To change attitudes towards Britain as a multicultural society, government needs to transform the public debate on race and immigration. The presentation of tough immigration policies as a condition for good race relations has inevitably triggered fears and hostility against ethnic minorities as well as towards legal immigrants and genuine asylum seekers.[284]

In order to compete in the global world, a new image needs to be fostered of Britain which celebrates its multiracial population and which can utilise the skills of its ethnic populations to win business from abroad. Asian businessmen are now going on government trade missions to East Africa and India in order to win orders for Britain. They know the languages and the ways of doing business in those places and it is the whole country which indirectly is benefiting from their skills. John Major's visit to India a few years ago, which had the support of British Asians, resulted in business deals worth three and a half billion pounds per year.[285] The enormous contribution of black Britons, particularly in the public sector and the world of arts, media and entertainment need to be similarly and regularly highlighted here and abroad. Other countries need to know modern Britain as a nation proud of its many people, not as a place hopelessly unable to move into modern, international times. In Canada the role played by entrepreneurs and other talented people of colour is referred to frequently by the government so that Canadians can learn to value multiculturalism for economic reasons and to feel that all Canadians make the nation proud.

It is only recently that organisations like the Commission For Racial Equality and political leaders have shifted their focus to the positive aspects of the transformations that this society has been through as a result of recent immigration. But the general population remains ignorant of the historical and contemporary contribution of ethnic communities to the economic, cultural and social life of this country. In July 1998, for example, Jack Straw acknowledged that the Asian community contributed £50 billion to the economy. The speech was made to the Asian business network and was not picked up by the main news outlets.[286]

> which means that this astonishing information is still unknown even by the elite in this country.

Where efforts are made to communicate such facts to people, attitudes are indeed affected. In Leicester extraordinary forms of regeneration have taken place since large numbers of East African Asians settled there in the Seventies. Leicester City once put out newspaper advertisements discouraging ethnic minorities from settling there at the time when there was an influx of dispossessed people from Uganda and other East African countries. Twenty five years later, 11 per cent of the jobs in the area have been created by these immigrants. Now, local authorities, the Chamber of Commerce and other local agencies accept with pride that multiculturalism is one of the most positive characteristics of their city.[287] Tourists are increasingly attracted to the city to sample Asian food and many of the local cricket clubs say that without their Asian membership they would have gone out of business.

There are clear steps which government could take to address negative attitudes and inject greater balance into the debate:

- Avoid making statements based on the assumption that good race relations depend on tough immigration policies. Instead, the rationale for immigration policies and regulations should be based on the particular context and reasons which are relevant to those policies and regulations.

- Acknowledge that Britain has been a country of immigration and that immigration has been the lifeblood of this nation which has brought benefits in every walk of life for centuries. This would help to change the negative view that many white people have of immigration and immigrants.

- Provide positive information about the contributions made by immigrants to this country and link these to the lives of ethnic individuals born here. Every successful black or Asian Briton born here is the descendant of an immigrant.

- Change the image of an immigrant so that the public do not associate the word with problems and burdens but with enterprise, ambition, courage and skills. There is no reason why white immigrants to the new world should be described as creative and hard working and why visible communities who came to Britain are still described within the problem paradigm.

- Avoid unnecessary inflammatory and emotive language when discussing immigration. To replace 'bogus' with 'abusive' is not helpful. 'Ineligible' would be a better description of people who fail to meet the strict criteria of the Geneva Convention. There is some evidence that Home Office press releases are avoiding the kind of rhetoric which was common under the last government. Words like 'scroungers' and statements like 'this country is not a honeypot' no longer appear which is to be welcomed.

- Provide accurate information about refugees and asylum seekers.

We need to have success stories of refugees who have settled and who are now key members of the community. What is also needed is information of refugees going back home after exile – like the many black and white anti-apartheid fighters who have returned and do have a great sense of loyalty to this country which will play out in trade and other important relationships.

- Explain to the British people that only a minority of those who fail in their applications are cheating the system. The rest simply do not qualify. There is now a widely held view that people who do not gain the right of abode are cheats and liars. This is surely unfair and unsound. Some who apply for asylum are indeed lying. But many do not meet the strict criteria which would give them refugee status and others fail to meet the exacting demands of our own regulations because they do not know them as well as they need to before they come here.

- Provide information on countries experiencing upheavals There is for example, factual information coming out of the Home Office which provides updated accounts of countries going through strife. It is essential to explain to people that even if people have a genuine case, a country as small and highly populated as this cannot be as open as conscientious politicians would like it to be. This is a different message from talking about costs to taxpayers and 'abusive' asylum seekers.

- Try to create a fairer system for dealing with applicants for asylum. Detention centres have been criticised and there is a human rights issue when people who have not been convicted or accused of any crime are treated as criminals.

- Appeal to the generous instincts of the British public. There is increasing concern in Britain about the way asylum seekers are treated. The IPPR survey into attitudes showed that there may be a mistaken assumption of hostility on the part of politicians and that there is scope to tap into the feelings of sections of the population who want to do more to help asylum seekers.

- Relocate the discourse on race relations. The issue needs to be placed within the context of the devolved United Kingdom, the new British nation, Europe, human rights and citizenship.

Ethnicity is important to all the tribes of the nation and to Europeans and it is up to the government to make sure that there is something which binds people in spite of these differences. There is no majority group in Europe and great ethnic variation therefore it may be time to reassess terms like 'ethnic minority' which may no longer be a useful way of describing modern European societies.

The material produced by the government to put across the message should also be inclusive and feature all the different people who make up Britain today. The multicultural project should be made as important to white people as it is to ethnic minorities. Messages which show real relationships between the different groups, mixed race families and future scenarios where black and white children no longer have any racial or cultural barriers would be a way forward. Located within the three key themes of the new Labour government – modernisation, social cohesion and personal responsibility – the campaign could be given added energy.

Strategies for action in the UK

This section contains proposals on how the UK government could influence public attitudes towards minorities and multicultural Britain. The recommendations include a fundamental reassessment of the way in which race relations and immigration policy have been presented in this country as well as ideas which can be implemented more immediately.

It would be a mistake to opt only for the easier modifications and leave the larger issues untouched because, as has already been argued, some long settled axioms, concepts and policies have been directly responsible for some of the negative attitudes of many in the majority community. This strategy will only work if endemic problems of poverty, structural inequality and racial discrimination are seen as priority areas for attention. This is not a strategy which seeks to change perceptions in isolation or suggests that this can ever be a substitute for changes in the law and other key areas essential for the promotion of an inclusive society. The work of the Social Exclusion Unit, planned work with families, New Deal and early education initiatives all need to take on board the problem of racial and religious prejudice as well as discrimination. It is, however beyond the scope of this document to go into these crucial policy areas.

At a local level conflict resolution work can be carried out by statutory and other agencies involved in various schemes. Going in to a housing estate to deal with racial prejudice may be less productive than going in to help with other problems and then incorporating the racial tensions into the work. In deprived areas, people often vent their very real problems and frustrations by scapegoating the 'other'. Rae Sibbit, in her Home Office report on perpetrators of racial harassment and violence describes some excellent initiatives which tackle prejudices born out of these frustrations and suggests that these could be emulated elsewhere.[288] These initiatives would have a much greater impact if the broader context was also taken up as a challenge by the government.

The strategy for this is divided into four broad categories:

- Government leadership and policy review

- Research

- Including the public in the process of change

- Communications and information strategy

Government leadership and policy review

In 1997, the CRE chairman, Sir Herman Ouseley challenged political leaders to promote positively the idea of fair, just and equal multiracial society.[289] Since Labour came to power, the Immigration Minister Mike O'Brien and Home Secretary Jack Straw have taken up this task with conviction. Both men have made a number of speeches about the pride they feel in multiracial Britain. They have also regularly been expressing the view that minorities have contributed enormously to life in this country. In November 1997, for example, it was the 25th anniversary of the arrival of Ugandan Asians in Britain after they had been forced to leave by Idi Amin. Mike O'Brien made a number of speeches on how this dispossessed community had become a significant economic asset to this country although neither of the key Ministers were able to attend the deeply symbolic service organised by Ugandan Asians to commemorate that period and to thank those Britons who had welcomed them.

The government should make it clear to the British population that it is determined to take responsibility to ensure that society is not fragmented along racial and religious lines and to build cohesive communities where attitudes towards diversity are positive. One senior Home Office official believes that what is needed is a 'people's movement to reject racism.' Bhikhu Parekh believes such a change needs bold action:

> Even if all racial discrimination were to end tomorrow, this would still be a society in which minorities lacked equal opportunities or felt legitimate, resented and marginalised. The law is bound to be ineffective unless it is embedded in and constantly nurtured by a broad campaign against the deeper roots of a discriminatory culture. Integration requires determined collective effort ... the government clearly has a role to play in providing moral leadership.[290]

The message needs to be sent and reinforced to the public that after a long period of neglect by previous governments, this Government is prepared to take the country forward so that it is at ease with multiracism and proud of its diversity. Our survey into attitudes indicated that many respondents felt that government leadership, together with the impact of the media, were central to how people's perceptions grow and change. As with the environment, people must be enabled to understand that the government regards a cohesive, multicultural society as central to its vision.

The Prime Minister should lead on this strategy and the initiative needs to be promoted and co-ordinated by the Cabinet Office. A number of special advisors consulted for this report are convinced that if Tony Blair led on this, the issue would be taken as seriously as the environment is now. At present, it is the Home Office which has the main responsibility for community relations policy as well as for the area of policy which has created the greatest difficulty within that area, that on immigration and asylum. Among the many officials and political advisors interviewed for this project, one asked an important question:

If with the drink driving campaigns we had government laws forbidding drink driving, and Ministers saying that the alcohol industry was central to this country's prosperity; and then we had education campaigns and speeches emphasising both the dangers of alcohol and the need to support the drink industry, what would the public think and do? In this country we tell the people that we need tight laws in order to reduce the problems that immigrants and refugees create; we pass laws to keep them out. We then also tell them that immigrants bring prosperity and they must not attack them. The same Ministers often praise immigrants, say we should not attack them and then talk of them treating this country as a honeypot.

The different approach of these two sections of the Home Office should be the first issue to be tackled. As Sarah Spencer has argued, government departments need:

> to sing the same tune. It is futile for the race relations section of the Home Office to be promoting positive approaches if the Immigration and Nationality department or Customs are creating a very different impression.[291]

Moreover, with the exception of the Department for Education and Employment which has a clear role in relation to promoting equality of opportunity in education and employment policy, government departments which could promote government policy in this area have not done so. The Department of Trade and Industry, with its knowledge of the contribution made by black entrepreneurs, of the contribution made by Asian businessmen in securing trade, and of the contribution to export earnings made by overseas students for instance, could make a significant contribution to redressing the terms of public debate. Consultations with individuals in this department suggest that there is political will at the highest level which could be used to encourage such a development. Peter Mandleson has spoken publicly about how he admired the ethnic diversity among the top people he met in Silicon Valley on an official trip and there is at present an action plan in place, led by the Permanent Secretary to promote racial equality in the department. The Ministry of Defence could highlight the contribution which has been made, and continues to be made by black and Asian soldiers as well as focusing on the need to eliminate racism and discrimination within the forces. The Scottish Office could draw attention to the contribution made by minorities north of the border.

There is thus not only a need for the Home Office to speak with one voice but for the government as a whole to promote the same approach: hence the Cabinet Office role in co-ordinating the government's strategy. As in Canada, every department could be expected to provide information annually to parliament on the specific contribution it has made to promoting the ideals of multiculturalism.[292]

The appointment of black and Asian Britons as special advisors and press officers, as well as within other key positions, would improve the communication of race and immigration issues. Their experiences and perceptions should inform Government policy and presentation. This argument has been accepted by the Labour government for women. And yet a recent *Guardian* article on people who were most influential officially and unofficially in the Labour government revealed that not one person was from the ethnic communities.[293] Real drive is now required to recruit talented individuals from the communities – preferably not those who describe themselves as representatives – who can provide a positive input into the thinking and communications strategy of the government. The Race Forum should be used to agree an action plan on this and to monitor progress. Details should be provided about all informal key appointments to the Forum. Since special advisors are influential and usually offered jobs without the usual procedures, opportunities exist to bring in black and Asian people – especially young people – into the inner circles of New Labour.

The Home Office should have responsibility for developing the strategy and develop appropriate training for key personnel. All relevant departmental Communications Directors should be co-opted and asked to contribute to an ongoing in-service training programme. The Home Office should organise seminars for speech writers, political advisors and others with influence. Ministers across the board must provide support and give the policy status.

The Home Office has in the past effectively delegated responsibility for promoting positive attitudes towards minorities to the Commission for Racial Equality (CRE). In recent years the CRE has given some priority to that task and adopted a number of different strategies from poster campaigns (with the assistance of Saatchi and Saatchi), a book and exhibition on the contribution made by minorities and migrants to life in the UK,[294] public events like its Race in the Media awards and well publicised campaign on racism in football. Our insistence that government itself must address public opinion reflects no criticism of the way in which the CRE has fulfilled this role, nor are we suggesting that it should pull back from that responsibility in future. Rather, we are suggesting that government itself must be seen to exercise leadership in this area because of its unique role as representatives of the nation as a whole. The CRE should complement the leadership tone set by government, not replace it.

Research

The public debate on immigration and on multiculturalism needs to be informed by better information. There is a paucity of facts and figures, particularly on immigration. There needs to be greater understanding, for instance, about why certain people are suddenly arriving and seeking refuge. Until 1995, Algerians barely came to this country. Since then a number of them have arrived seeking asylum. Regular, updated information must be provided on the changing scene and stereotypes should be dispelled. The public should know, for example, that government sponsored research found that refugees who have settled in the UK are more highly qualified and skilled people than the indigenous population.

The government should regularly inform the public about the contributions which the visible minorities make and how important this has been to the country through history. In contrast to immigration, there is now a substantial body of research into the lives of ethnic minorities in Britain, but most of it is focused on negative experiences like discrimination, racial violence or the issue of identity. There is little clearly research available which provides data to support a positive integration policy and important information remains unknown.

How many know, for example, that the Indian food trade in this country now has a larger turnover than steel, coal and shipbuilding and that chicken tikka is one of Marks and Spencer's biggest exports?[295] Are they aware not only that we have successful Asian businessmen but that in the food industry alone, according to DEMOS, 70,000 jobs have been created by these businessmen.[296] Such information should be drawn together by government departments and used to inform the public and redress misconceptions. The Department of Health could commission a study on the role and impact of black and Asian doctors in the National Health Service; the Department for Education and

Employment could provide statistics on the number of high-flying ethnic minority science graduates. Disseminating information to the general public would be an essential component of the new strategy.

Some areas of ignorance need to be tackled as a matter of urgency by local and national governments. Most people do not know how much racial violence there is in this country or why it happens. The excellent Home Office report on the perpetrators of racial violence and abuse[297] has not been made as well known as it should be. The Runnymede Trust's report on Islamaphobia[298] shows a growing level of ignorance about hostility towards Muslims. Accurate information needs to come from government on the British Muslim community which is the largest visible minority in this country. Most of the time the public image of this community as portrayed by the media is negative and ill-informed. This is causing great disaffection among young Muslims and government has a responsibility to redress the balance which would reassure both Muslims and non-Muslims.[299]

Factual booklets could be published on this and other areas of ignorance. This was done when, for example, the Foreign and Commonwealth Office published *Facts and Fairytales Revisited*, a well produced booklet on the European Union.[300]

Information like the statistics on black 'muggers' needs to be provided in context with other figures, providing a racial breakdown of other kinds of crime. If we were informed not only that 'mugging' in some areas is mainly carried out by small groups of young black men but that rape and burglaries are more likely to be committed by white criminals, the presentation of the information could not be said to be biased. The government should present information likely to cause alarm with sensitivity. It must liaise with black and Asian people working in the particular field to ensure that the right information – however unpalatable – is put across but in a way that builds consensus. It is important that there is trust between the Government and black and Asian Britons so that problems within these communities can be discussed with politicians.[301] This is more likely to happen if balanced information is provided by the Government. There are too many issues at present that are not openly discussed because of fears of reactions like those which have greeted the publication of figures on crimes committed by black people. This does not benefit either black or Asian Britons or the Government.[302]

Immigration

We recommend that a programme of research on immigration issues should be initiated by the Home Office. Key areas to explore include the social and economic impact of immigration and the effect of existing controls. In Germany, for example, economists at Essen produced figures in 1993 showing what economic gains West Germany had made from the labour of migrant workers. They calculated that, had these workers not arrived after the war, West Germans would have paid more in taxes.[303] In Australia such research has enabled officials to brief journalists and to improve the quality of the debate on immigration, necessary in recent years when there has been growing concern over Asian migrants. In North America, also, research has been able to show that immigrants pay higher taxes and received less in welfare services than did non-immigrants.[304]

Carrying out such research in the UK would enable the issue of immigration to be discussed in a more informed and less emotive way. It would make it possible for government to counteract misconceptions and myths and thereby, over time, to change the public discourse on immigration.

Government research should be carried out to evaluate the impact of immigration policies on race relations and some of this work needs to be done in areas where there are high levels of tensions between diverse communities.

White identities and attitudes

White Britons are not a homogenous group. The diversity of opinion, emerging identities, attitudes to racial minorities and multiculturalism within the majority community needs to be studied. Research into this 'new' area should be instigated by the Government. There is a need to find out, for instance, what influences attitudes to wards multiculturalism if a strategy to influence those attitudes is to be successful.

The government should sponsor ongoing in depth studies on attitudes towards minorities in Britain in order to track what is happening in particular geographical locations, during economic boom periods, during recessions, among the young, and so forth. The various manifestations of negative attitudes need to be better studied. Research on public opinion is carried out for the government in many policy areas.

The practice should be extended to this issue as Home Office Report.

Involving the public

People need to engage with these re-definitions so that they do not feel that the political elite is imposing their own view. Focus groups should be organised to launch nation wide discussions within the framework of civic responsibilities, citizenship values and modern Britain.

The current government has developed a framework for public consultation with its People's Panel. Race, immigration and multiculturalism should be included in that process. Using and adapting some of the techniques developed in Canada and some of the good practice in the UK, the government should conduct public consultation exercises to test opinion on immigration and asylum legislation and other controversial measures. This would make the policies more informed and more consensual. It would also create a new trust between policy makers and the British people, many of whom feel resentful that their views on these subjects are not taken seriously.

Public information, education and communication strategies

It is valuable to look at information campaigns which have been organised on issues unrelated to multiculturalism to see what lessons can be learned. Although racial attitudes are complex and in many ways particular, it would be a mistake to imagine that the approach used to influence attitudes in other areas would always be inappropriate. There is, after all, near-universal agreement, in principle, that racism is undesirable and unjust and that racial and ethnic prejudice is damaging to society.

Several interviews were carried out for this project with individuals working for advertising companies who had previously or were presently involved in public education campaigns for the government or government agencies. The author also met with the manager at the Central Office for Information and his team as well as with the Communications Director for the Commission for Racial Equality. Press officers and Communications Directors from three Government departments were also consulted. The aim of these consultations was to establish the factors which contributed to effective campaigns. Some fundamental principles emerged out of these discussions:

- Messages are more effective if they are not too clearly perceived as coming from interested parties and if they do not focus too much on negative aspects. This was the lesson learnt, for instance, from the anti-drugs campaigns in the 1980, which used young models who looked tired, thin and ill. Research revealed that some teenagers were actually attracted by the posters and the television messages and images.[305]

- Sometimes indirect challenges to stereotypes have a stronger impact. The cast of Eastenders, for example, gives a more real and realistic 'education' on the new British identity than can any expensive professional campaign.

- The most effective messages have a clear target, where the theoretical framework and leverage has been established and where a multi-layered, inter-agency approach can be worked out.

- Most of the people interviewed stressed that adequate time and sufficient resources need to be made available if attitudes are to be changed. Campaigns need to be phased and evaluated.

- Campaigns need to be constantly supported by politicians and other opinion leaders and the messages should not be in any way contradictory or confused.

- Campaigns which are aspirational do have more impact than those which simply 'threaten' or reveal negative truths. The green issue is now better understood and supported than a decade ago. The professional advertisers interviewed for this project agreed that the success of the green campaign could be attributed to the combination of fear and hope it invoked for the future of the world to be inherited by our children.

- The best intentioned government campaigns can go wrong – not least if competing with contradictory messages coming from other sources. With smoking for example, young people are not yet giving up in large numbers because films, magazines and role models do portray smoking as a glamorous activity.

It is instructive to look at some of the successful campaigns which have been waged to change attitudes and behaviour.

The drink driving campaign

The campaign was launched in 1967. It has been running continuously since then, even though figures of people killed as a result of drink driving have fallen from approximately 2,500 to 540 per annum. At present day prices, an average of three million pounds a year has been spent on this particularly effective education campaign. Proper resources and adequate time are important elements which have contributed to its success. Law enforcement, punishments which were a real deterrent, political will, the dissemination of factual evidence both of the consequences of drink driving and of the legal penalties, plus memorable advertisements have combined to create gradual changes in the social acceptability of drinking and driving.

Qualitative research by advertising companies prior to, and following, new campaigns contributed to ensuring that the right people were targeted and in the most effective way. Ongoing assessments are part of the process. Research indicated, for example, that young men were less fearful of dying than of being seriously disabled. They were also moved by the idea that their actions might harm the people they loved. Advertisements were then produced to fit the fear. Evaluations of recent campaigns show there is an 80 per cent recall of these adverts. Even companies selling alcohol have provided funds for public education campaigns to stop drink driving because they do not wish to be seen as socially irresponsible.[306]

Let's Kick Racism Out of Football

This campaign has been less well resourced than the drink driving campaign but like the latter there has been careful phasing over a considerable length of time. It was initiated by the CRE and others to eradicate racism from football in 1996. It is aimed at those white people who love the game.[307] The thrust of the campaign has been positive and inclusive. It is particularly appealing to the young and the pride which they want to feel in their teams and in the game. It has had unprecedented support from politicians. Leaflets tell people in the stadiums to take personal responsibility for reporting racists and the well produced glossy magazine *Kick It Again* seemed to capture the professional pride that fans feel.[308]

Other factors which have contributed to the success of the project:

- It has the backing of key star footballers and politicians, businessmen, football club board members, ordinary club members and the media. An Advisory Group Against Racism and Intimidation includes top players and ex-players, the Football Association, the Football Supporters Association, the League of Managers and the Association of Metropolitan Authorities.

- Black and white people are partners in this initiative.

- The handing over of responsibility for this to football clubs gave the messages more credibility than if the message had simply come from the Commission for Racial Equality. This ownership needs to be replicated in other areas of public life.

- The campaign has a long term view of the effect which it needs to achieve.

- It has operated on a local and national level.

Whilst highlighting the effects of racism, the campaign appeals to the fans through positive, not negative, images.

The Zero Tolerance campaign against domestic violence

The Edinburgh District Council Women's Committee funded the first Zero Tolerance campaign which aimed to change public attitudes towards domestic violence towards women. The uncompromising campaign title has since been adapted by the Labour government in other areas of public policy. In the initial Scottish campaign, however, five posters were used over a period of months. They included:

- A happy picture of two young sisters playing in a bedroom with the message, 'By the time they are 18 one of them will have been subjected to sexual abuse'

- A middle class woman with the message, 'She lives with a successful businessman, loving father and respected member of the community. Last week he hospitalised her.'

- An elderly woman with a young girl with a message saying that females from 3 to ninety three are raped within families.

Other posters asserted that men did not have the right to abuse women. This was hard-hitting material. At the same time as this, the local press was asked to run articles on each of the issues highlighted in the posters. An evaluation of the campaign showed that the messages had been seen and recall was high. There was also considerable support for the need to campaign in order to change these attitudes:

> There is a widespread feeling that campaigns of this nature are desperately needed and there is general support for the Zero Tolerance Campaign [and the possibility of other public awareness interventions of this type]. It is likely to be welcomed by the majority of the population in other regions or areas.[309]

Government can also learn from evidence emerging from other countries showing that advertising campaigns on television which set out to change public attitudes towards the visible minorities are most effective if:

●   They stress the positive aspects of ethnic minority lives, but only those which make them seem similar to the wider society.

●   They do not concentrate on negative messages about bad experiences which reinforce negative attitudes.

●   They use many examples rather than highlighting one individual – otherwise the interpretation is always individualised.

●   Messages are not implicit (which leaves the receiver too much power to interpret) but explicit and repeated many times over.[310]

Other researchers have argued that governments aiming to create deep cultural shifts in society require time and the continual reinforcement of messages through using different forms and mediums of communication with the public.[311]

The IPPR qualitative survey (detailed in chapter 2) asked people what kind of campaigns make a difference to attitudes. Many of the respondents felt that advertising messages which focused on the contributions of ethnic minorities rather than showing them as victims of racism would be more effective, as well as less humiliating to black and Asian Britons.

There is clearly much that the British government could learn from models of good practice in relation to non-race issues in the UK and to race issues abroad. Although a change in attitudes on race will take time because they are deeply held, fixed by history and tied in with concepts of national identity, the process is long overdue.

Key points of the strategy which the government should introduce the following ideas:

- It is essential that positive speeches are made to the public in general, not only to ethnic community audiences.

- Key, symbolic events should have high level government representation.

- Occasions which are of particular significance in Britain should be made more inclusive by the Government. Officials should ensure, for instance, that the memorial services to mark the end of the Second World War always include tributes to the millions of black and Asian soldiers who fought with the allies.

- This nation now consists of those who were once colonisers and their descendants as well as those who were colonised and their children. Care therefore needs to be taken about how the period of empire is described, what it meant and what the British nation is today. Old or new symbols need to be handled with sensitivity and some awareness of the effect on ethnic minority Britons.

- All Ministers should strive to include an acknowledgement of multiculturalism in their public speeches whenever appropriate. They should condemn clearly and assertively all those in parliament who make statements which could incite racial hostility.

- Problems should not be ignored – they must be addressed – but should be presented as part of a wider picture to avoid perpetuating a dominant 'problem perspective'.

- Public education campaigns built on partnerships and which take a long term view of the process of change can work remarkably well as has been shown by the well targeted *Kick Racism Out of Football* campaign.

- Campaigns need to be run over a long period, reinforcing the same message.

- Great care should be taken to avoid emotive language.

- Assertions about the impact of migrants on the UK should be based on fact.

Political leaders might consider using the word British with black, Asian and Chinese. African-Americans use this form with considerable pride and it makes a statement about their origins and their place in the United States. The term 'ethnic minority' is felt by many to do neither although, again, using the words 'British' or 'Britons' as a prefix or suffix would be a step forward. 'Fundamentalism' is a word used to discredit certain religious groups, in particular Muslims. This should be avoided. 'Extremism' would be a better word as it can be used for all sorts of groups, black and white.

To have real effect all government communication should be scrutinised for negative messages about ethnic minority Britons and should be produced to include the diverse populations which make up this nation.

The media

Governments cannot tell the media what to do but spin doctors have some influence on the output. If the government can influence the media and 'sell' other economic and social policies, there is no reason to believe that this cannot be done with race relations.[312] Other tactics used with great skill at present can be extended to cover this area. They include:

- Rebuttal teams should be set up to respond to misinformation in the media about race and immigration. All press and broadcasts on the Government are already carefully monitored. Immediate action is taken now on other issues to correct misinformation or misleading information.

- Press releases should be scrutinised by the Communications Director in the Home Office to ensure that various departments are not contradicting one another or giving muddled messages. This is something that is being considered by the Race Equalities Unit at the Home Office.[313]

- Journalists should be provided with facts, ideas and new approaches to get a more balanced view in the British media on immigration and race. This is not to censor material or manipulate the media. Sensitive information should not be withheld but must be presented with due care.

- The direct line between some Immigration Service officials and the sections of the press needs to be investigated and guidelines laid down. There needs to be more accountability established on who is sending material to the media and the authorisation of such material.

- Government press officers should have in place a checking and authorisation process – possibly located at the Home Office –to ensure that press releases minimise the dangers of misrepresentation.

- Proactive action is needed to get key government figures on the broadcast media to talk about race and multiculturalism on popular programmes.

New stories

At the heart of this strategy is the need to change the story about this nation, past and future. We need to change myths about a monocultural settled and idyllic population which was upset by the arrival of 'aliens'. Without immigration even the English would not have been here. The new blood which was injected into the country after the devastation of the two wars stopped from cultural in-breeding and economic stagnation. Black and Asian people have gained hugely from this experience too. There is no going back to the future for any of the groups who make up this island. But by re-imagining Britain for the future as a country rooted in history, good and bad, but not imprisoned by it a new vision can be created. Gordon Brown's quote at the beginning of this report shows we have started this new story.

Public occasions and symbolic events

In local authorities and at the CRE there is now agreement that there need to be rewards as well as punitive measures to promote good race relations. The CRE has said that it is keen on winning 'hearts and minds'.[314] One effective way in which they have done this is to initiate awards for various national activities. The occasions have acquired prestige and credibility. An example is the Race in the Media Awards where journalists and broadcasters are rewarded for sensitive and innovative coverage of race and multicultural issues. This is especially important to affect the attitudes of journalists who play such a key role in the images people receive. The Good Citizenship Awards and Local Authority Awards are similarly respected.

The government should follow these examples. The Prime Minister could present the prizes and use the occasion to make speeches on the themes of diversity and the new British nation. Ministers should make positive speeches about minority communities and multiculturalism to white audiences as well as to ethnic gatherings. Making speeches to the converted or interested parties has the important effect of reassuring and validating people. But to change attitudes other more resistant audiences need to be addressed in similar terms. Some of the speeches made at such events should be published in an attractive form and made available to the public. Key Government figures should be present at important multicultural events such as the Notting Hill Carnival.

When there are tragic events like the racist killing of Stephen Lawrence, public declarations should be made by the Government. Memorial events for such killings should have Ministerial representation. The appearance of a Home Office Minister with the family of Stephen Lawrence to mark the fifth anniversary of his death set an important precedent.

The Stephen Lawrence inquiry is seen by many as an immensely important symbolic gesture which has given a signal to black and white Britons that this Government takes racial injustice seriously. This acknowledgement should become the rule rather than the exception.

A final and central point. None of the above can be done without the allocation of resources. For the first time in decades the political will is not in doubt. Uniquely, all of the three party political leaders in this country are truly committed to a multiracial Britain. There is a real opportunity to transform attitudes so that finally the whole country can feel at ease with itself and take pride in the diversity of its people.

5. Conclusion

Britain is experiencing a national identity crisis. Public attitudes towards minorities and lack of acceptance of Britain as a multicultural nation are one key component of that mood of uncertainty and anxiety, that crisis of national self confidence, which Labour has set out to address. This book argues that, if Labour is to create the cohesive, integrated and self confident nation to which it aspires, it must address public attitudes towards minorities, and their integral position within British society, by adopting a deliberate, long-term, cross-departmental strategy to that end.

Chapter 1 acknowledged that Labour is already adopting a different approach from its predecessors. Clear signs have emerged that the Government recognises the need to make clear to white Britons, as well as to black, that Britain benefits from the contribution made by members of minorities in all walks of life. It recognised the need to avoid inflammatory language and is beginning to portray multiculturalism as a concept which embraces all members of society, not only people of colour. But there is still a necessity to transform its tentative steps into a coherent strategy.

Chapter 2 set out the evidence of social exclusion – in employment and unemployment, in levels of racial violence, in white hostility to inter-marriage and minority neighbours, in the alienation of black and Asian youth. The other side of the coin is the growing evidence of success – in the education system and at work, but the failure of white attitudes to keep pace with those developments, continuing to perceive minority communities generically as a problem. IPPR's own research exposed the connection between resentment towards minorities and wider anxieties about a perceive loss of white identity: that 'British' no longer held any clear meaning. As commentators concluded in the 1960s when the problems were first emerging, a society facing such major demographic and cultural changes needs strong and consistent political leadership to allay the fears which such change generates; leadership to portray a new vision of a modern, inclusive multicultural nation.

Chapter 3 traced the development in political and public responses to immigration from the 1950s to the current decade. It demonstrated how the terms of today's debate had their roots in the political compromise carved out in the 1960s: the appeasement of the section of white opinion hostile to immigration, coupled with legislative sanctions on discriminatory behaviour. The ambiguity in the attitudes of political leaders was reflected in the contradictions found by researchers in the attitudes of members of the public; overt racism in a minority, a tolerance in others which could have been nursed by strong and unequivocal leadership, but was not. Politicians manifestly had an impact on public opinion, but did not use it to good effect. Even when the Conservative government of the early 1970s did decide to honour its obligations to the Ugandan refugees, holders of British passports, it did so with such reluctance that the signal which it sent to the public was clear.

If ever-tightening immigration controls were designed to reassure the public, they undoubtedly failed to do so. Public concern about immigration remained high, government failed to redress misinformation in the press, an absence of research precluded informed debate.

Towards the end of the last government's term of office, a noticeable shift in the tone of some speeches could be detected. The contribution which minorities have made to British society was acknowledged and praised. But the audience was most often the minority communities themselves and the message did not always ring true when the reality of immigration control, on friends and relatives, told a different story.

Chapter 4 showed that a new approach is needed. It argued that the government's goal should be public acceptance of an inclusive multiculturalism, lying at the heart of their confidence in Britain's modern, national identity: a multiculturalism that does not lie at the margins of white society but encompasses it. Whites, too, are multicultural and should equally be encouraged to feel pride in their varied cultural heritage. A strategy which focuses not on special treatment for minorities (although any section of society may need assistance from time to time) but on shared involvement within a national project.

In order to achieve that goal, the government should devise a deliberate strategy to lead public opinion, to transform the terms of public debate on race and on immigration. Drawing attention to the contribution which minorities make – to trade, to the creation of jobs, to cultural life and to so many other areas would help to redress the imbalance in current perceptions. Avoiding inflammatory language, explaining the rationale for immigration policy, stressing respect and acceptance rather than tolerance, were some of the many suggestions made for the message which government should seek to put across.

There are some examples of good practice abroad, innovative ideas from which we could learn in Canada, the Netherlands and Berlin. The Canadian model in particular had much to offer: the acceptance of responsibility across government to promote an integrated strategy; the emphasis on the commonality of citizenship, stressing mutual rights and responsibilities; the successful re-evaluation of multiculturalism as an inclusive concept, a central part of Canada's national identity, with identifiable benefits for the country as a whole; and the symbolic use of Citizenship ceremonies to reinforce within individual Citizens the responsibilities and rights which that status confers.

In advocating a new strategy for the UK, the government must first identify its goal – the kind of multicultural Britain to which it aspires. Secondly, it must clarify its message and make the necessary internal arrangements to ensure that that message is conveyed by Ministers and officials across government. The message must be clear and consistent. The public should understand that the government regards a cohesive, multicultural society as central to its vision. The Prime Minister should take the lead and implementation of the strategy be co-ordinated and monitored by a unit in the Cabinet Office. The Home Office would remain the lead department, spearheading the initiative; its first responsibility being to ensure that its own Immigration and Nationality Department brought the presentation of immigration policy into line with the rest of the government's strategy.

Individuals from ethnic communities should be part of the team devising the strategy and among the senior officials, and staff of press offices, which deliver it. The CRE should retain its own responsibility to address attitudes but should complement the lead taken by government, not replace it.

The strategy needs to be informed by research into the impact of immigration and into the contribution made by members of minorities, to give the government the information it will need to educated the public and counter misinformation. Factual information should be made widely available as it has, for instance, to dispel the myths about the European Union. Sensitive information, such as that on the involvement of black people in crime, should be presented in context to ensure that the public receive a balanced picture. The aim should not be to withhold information which highlights problems but to ensure that the public do not receive that message in isolation. In no case is this more important than in relation to immigration.

If the Government is to change attitudes it must have detailed information on the attitudes which different groups of people hold and the grounds on which they hold those views. It must also conduct research to find out by what means and which argument it can most effectively encourage people to question their own attitudes. The Government should engage the public in the exercise of redefining multiculturalism by leading an open debate. It should not be afraid to have a public discussion but should lead and inform it.

The Government could learn from successful information campaigns which have been run on non-race related issues, such as that on drink-driving. Many of the lessons from such campaigns, to some of which I referred, could be applied to this campaign – not least that it would have to be conducted over a long period to be effective.

Finally, there are some suggestions for the many approaches government could use in its communications strategy from attendance at symbolic events to its use of language: it should set up a media rebuttal team to respond to misinformation in the media on race or immigration issues, responding immediately on these issues as it already does on so many others; press releases should be scrutinised to ensure a consistency of message; journalists provided with facts and human interest stories which balance the negative content of so many of the stories which they choose to cover; sensitive information should not be withheld but handled with care. Implementation of the strategy will require some allocation of resources, but mostly requires simply the political will. No that the leaders of the three largest political parties in the country are united in their commitment to a multicultural society, there is a unique opportunity to unite the public behind an new, inclusive vision of Britain and what it means to be British. The Government should seize the moment and act now.

Endotes

1. *The Guardian,* 12 November 1998.

2. In *Five Views of Multi-Racial Britain*, Commission For Racial Equality and the BBC, 1978, p29.

3. *The Guardian,* 15 October 1997.

4. Personal Communication.

5. Quoted by Y Alibhai-Brown, in *The Independent*, 31 May 1996.

6. This was evident in the speech made by Lord Tebbit at the Tory party conference in October 1997 when he said that ethnic minority Britons could not be truly of this nation unless they imbibed British values and history. Interestingly most of the prominent Tories and the media did not support these views and for the first time in recent history, the speech seemed out of tune and out of touch with modern times and the views of most British people. William Hague responded to the sentiment expressed by Tebbit in forceful terms. See the press coverage of the week 3-10 October.

7. A quote from a Radio 4 programme during the week of 19 April 1991.

8. M/029/97, The Labour Party.

9. *Britain's Just Got Better! Thanks to You*, B/024/97, The Labour Party, May 1997.

10. Bernie Grant MP, Darcus Howe and many others protested against this. See the *Sunday Telegraph*, 20 April 1997.

11. *Creative Britain*, Faber, 1998, pp22-23.

12. *Ibid*, p37.

13. See the texts of the speeches made to conference on the 3 October 1995 and the 1 October 1996. This quote is on p12 in the 1996 speech.

14. Full text in *The Guardian* 1 October 1997.

15. See Keith Vaz, *The Class Ceiling* October 1997, and *Whitehall Remaining White*, May 1998.

16. Speech to the Singapore Business Community, 8 January 8 1996, text in *The Guardian* 9 September 1996.

17. Speech made in Coventry, 14 November at the Attitudes to Race conference organised by the City Council.

18. *The Battle over Britain*, Demos, London, 1995, p13.

19. *The Independent*, 19 June 1996.

20. See for example, *The Evrigenis Report*, European Parliament, December 1985, p72.

21. OJ C 289/148 5 November 1992, Response to a written question in the European Parliament.

22. *Ibid,* pp89-90.

23. European Commission (88) 318, p2.

24. European Commission Communication 24 03 03, 25 February 1994.

25. *Ibid,* Foreword.

26. See the Chapter on attitudes in the study by EJB Rose and associates, Oxford University Press, 1969.

CHAPTER 2

27. See the text of his lecture at the University of Sheffield published in *The Guardian*, 26 January 1994.

28. *Britain TM*, (Demos, 1997) by Mark Leonard, confirms this national sense of unease.

29. See Michael Ignatieff, 'Who Are We Now?' in *Prospect*, April 1998.

30. K Malik, *The Meaning of Race*, Macmillan, 1996, p12.

31. *'The Rights we Enjoy Reflect the Duties we Owe'*, *The Spectator Lecture*, 22 March 1995.

32. *The Independent*, 3 July 1995.

33. See the warnings in The Commission For Racial Equality Annual Report, 1995.

34. See for example, Y Alibhai-Brown, Fear and Loathing in Southall, *The Independent*, 6 June 1995.

35. See for example the government reactions to the report submitted by Liberty to the United Nations Committee in April 1997 quoted in *The Scotsman* 4 March 1996. The Home Office Minister said that Britian had a 'proud record' on race relations and that 'our race relations policies are second to none.'

36. See Trevor Phillip's 'Fantastic Voyage', in *The Guardian* 17 May 1998 in which he describes his television series on black Britons fifty years since the arrival of Windrush. The programmes shows how much has been achieved by this community and how they are now an integral and indispensable part of the British Landscape.

37. Information in various chapters in *Diversity and Disadvantage: The Ethnic Minorities in Britain*, T Modood, R Berthoud *et al*, Policy Studies Institute, 1997.

38. Reported in *The Observer*, 17 November 1996.

39. See C Peach, *Ethnicity in the 1991 Census*, Vol 2, *The Ethnic Minority Populations of Great Britain*, HMSO, June 1996.

40. See for example PE Ogden, 'Immigration to France since 1945: Myth and Reality', *Ethnic and Racial Studies* Vol 14, No 3, July 1991.

41. Modood, Berthoud *et al, op cit* pp63-75.

42. Commission For Racial Equality, *Roots for the Future*, 1996.

43. *Ibid.* p v.

44. Labour Party Conference Figures published in *Black to Black*, Issue 10, September 1996.

45. See *The Guardian*, 1 October 1997, p9.

46. See *Whitehall Remaining White*, May 1998.

47. *Incomes of Ethnic Minorities*, University of Essex, 1998.

48. See for example reports in *The Independent*, 12 June 1996 of the findings of the Office For National Statistics published in the same month.

49. Quoted in *The Guardian*, 4 February 1997.

50. Details in Modood, Berthoud *et al, op cit*.

51. *Racial Abuse: An everyday experience for some Londoners*, 1993.

52. In *Racial Violence: A Separate Offence? A Discussion Paper*, The All-Party Parliamentary Group on Race and Community, House of Commons, 1994, p1.

53. See R Hewitt, Sagaland: *Youth Culture, Racism and Education: A report on research carried out in Thamesmead*, London Borough of Greenwich/University of London, 1986. Also M Fitzgerald and C Hale, *Ethnic Minorities: victimisation and racial harassment*, Home Office Research Study 154, 1996.

54. Modood, Berthoud *et al, op cit* p 288.

55. *Racial Violence: A separate offence?* Houses of Parliament, 1993/94, p1.

56. Dr Rae Sibbitt, Home Office research study, No 176, 1997, p101.

57. *The Independent*, 2 February 1997.

58. See press reports for example of racism in Yeovil, Somerset, 2 February 1996. See also report on rural racism in reports by the CRE in 1996.

59. A forthcoming report collating information presented at an IPPR seminar on divided communities deals in depth with this issue.

60. See Fred Halliday, *Islam and the Myth of Confrontation*, IB Taurus, 1995.

61. *Islamophobia, Its Features and Dangers, A Consultative Paper*, Runnymede Trust, February 1997, p7.

62. S Huntington, *The Clash of Civilisations?* Foreign Affairs, Summer 1993.

63. *The Spectator* 19 October 1991.

64. *The Times* 11 May 1989.

65. *The Times* 21 April 1995.

66. *International Herald Tribune*, 9 November 1993.

67. Draft chapter of Halliday's book on Islam and the west, Chapter 4, p3. See also Halliday's published *Islam and the Myth of Confrontation*, IB Taurus, 1995, Chapter 4.

68. *A Very Light Sleeper*, Runnymede Trust, January 1994, p12.

69. *Ibid* p9.

70. Reports in *The Herald*, 28 September 1996.

71. Report in *The Jewish Chronicle*, 6 August 1993.

72. Suzanne Glass in *Real Life*, *The Independent on Sunday*, 4 June 1995.

73. 7 August 1994.

74. Gallup poll, September 1993, quoted in *A Very Light Sleeper*, *op cit* p50.

75. In *Essays and Speeches*, Edited by Anthony Lester, Collins, 1967 .

76. Speech to Labour Party Home Affairs Group made on 11 June 1996.

77. See for example, H.Shuman et al, *Racial Attitudes in America - Trends and Interpretations,* Harvard University Press, 1997.

78. When the IPPR surveys were published, a letter by Jenny Bourne from the Institute of Race Relations published in *The Guardian* (7 February 1997) objected vehemently to such research.

79. August 8 1995.

80. This was the view of many in the ethnic press following publication of the IPPR data in February 1997.

81. See for example Les Back, *Racist name calling and developing anti-racist initiatives in youth work*, Warwick Centre for Research in Ethnic Relations, 1990, Paper 14, and also Roger Hewitt, *Routes to Racism*, Institute of Education, 1996.

82. *Racial Discrimination in Britain,* Pelican 1968, p83.

83. 5 May 1995.

84. 8 August 1995.

85. Keith Vaz, MP was quoted in *The Daily Express* on 8 August 1995 saying that he was 'very surprised' by the results.

86. BBC Radio Five Live/Harris Poll, 20 May 1996.

87. Music TV/Scantel survey published in January 1997.

88. 12th Report, R Jowell *et al,* Social and Community Planning Research, 1997.

89. *The Independent* 21 November 1996.

90. T Modood, R Berthoud *et al, op cit,* 1997, in various chapters.

91. European Commission, Brussels, November 1989 and November 1997.

92. See 'Death in Somerstown', in *Mindfield: The Race Issue,* Camden press, 1998.

93. Oxford University Press, 1969, p737.

94. D Nandy, *Race as Politics in Towards an Open Society: Ends and Means in British Politics,* Pemberton Books, 1971, pp122-30.

95. *The Observer,* 13 October 1991.

96. Speech made at a Justice organised conference on human rights, 15 June 1995.

97. National Identity and the ontological regeneration of Britain, in *Culture, Markets and Nation,* (ed) A Gilbert and P Gregory, Avesbury, 1995 p93.

98. Published February 1998, the report revealed that surveys indicated eight out of ten Europeans did not have adequate information about the EU.

99. Personal communication with the then special advisor to Douglas Hurd in the FCO.

CHAPTER 3

100. 23 June 1948.

101. Pluto Press, 1984, p372.

102. *Hansard,* 7 July 1948, col 405.

103. PRO HO 213/244 22 June 1948.

104. PRO CO 876/88, 5 July 1948.

105. *The Meaning of Race*, Macmillan, 1996, p19.

106. See *Invisible Empire: racism in Canada*, Random House 1995.

107. See Zig Layton Henry, *The Politics of Race in Britain*, Allen and Unwin, 1984, pp32-33.

108. 1955 Cabinet Papers quoted in *The Guardian*, 12 January 1986 Further details also appeared in *The Times*, 1 January 1992 and *The Guardian* 2 January 1992.

109. Cape, 1959.

110. *The Colour problem*, Harmondsworth, 1955.

111. In PB Rich, *Race and Empire in British Politics*, Cambridge University Press, 1986, pp179-182.

112. Ruth Glass, *Newcomers: The West Indians In London*, Allen and Unwin, 1960.

113. *The Colour Problem*, Harmondsworth 1955, pp245-246. See also the analysis of P Rich, *Race and Empire in British Politics*, *op cit*, pp181-182 .

114. P Foot, *Immigration and Race in British Politics*, Penguin, 1965, pp233-234.

115. *Ibid*.

116. For a detailed account of this and the way police and others handled the crisis see Fryer, *op ci*t chapter 11.

117. See R Glass, *op cit*.

118. See details of this and other acts of racial antagonism in Fryer, *op cit*. pp376-379.

119. See for example his essay '*British racism: the road to 1984*' in *Race and Class*, Vol XXV Autumn 1983, No 2 .

120. Cited in J Rutherford, *Forever England*, Lawrence and Wishart, September 1997.

121. *Coloured People from British Colonial Territories*, CP 50 113, 18 May.

122. Z Layton-Henry, 1984, *op cit* pp28-29.

123 This work was carried out in 1996 over a period of three months. Interviews were taped and extracts summarised for this study.

124. Z Layton-Henry, *The Politics of Immigration*, Blackwell, 1992, p67.

125. This was described by many of the interviewees interviewed for this project. See the introduction. Two erstwhile white supervisors of factories in Walsall confirmed to the author that this was common practice.

126. For details of this see Fryer, *op cit* Chapter 11.

127. See the Introduction in Y Alibhai-Brown and A Montague, *The Colour of Love*, Virago, 1992.

128. J Rose *et al*, *Colour and Citizenship*, OUP 1969, p214.

129. For a full account See Z Layton-Henry, *The Politics of Immigration*, Blackwell, 1992.

130. Cited in Hansard vol 596, col.1563, 5 December 1958.

131. Labour Party, *Racial Discrimination*, September 1958.

132. Z Layton-Henry, 1984, *op cit* p51.

133. P Foot, *op cit*, p232.

134. See Rose *et al*, table 28.24.

135. *Hansard*, 3 May 1965, col 977-978.

136. *Race and Empire in British Politics, op cit* p200.

137. Quoted in John Solomos, *Race and Racism in Contemporary Britian*, Macmillan, 189, p50.

138. *Race and Politics in Britain*, Harvester Wheatsheaf, p175.

139. *Ethnic Pluralism in Britain: The Demographic and Legal Background*, in *Ethnic Pluralism and Public Policy*, (ed) Nathan Glazer and Ken Young, Heinemann/PSI 1983, pp48-49.

140. P Foot, *op cit* p172.

141. Z Layton-Henry,1984, *op cit* p55.

142. *Ibid* p57.

143. R Crossman *Diaries of a Cabinet Minister*, vol 2, Hamish Hamilton 1975, p149.

144. *Ibid* p299.

145. *Racial Discrimination in Britain*, Pelican, London 1968.

146. J Rose *et al*, 1969, *op cit* p736.

147. *The Spectator*, 1 March 1968.

148. *Hansard* 4 March 1976, col 1605.

149. See A Dummett and M Dummett, 'The Role of Government in Britain's Racial Crisis', in *Justice First*, Sheed and Ward, (ed) L Donnelly, 1969.

150. See the debate of 23 April 1968 on the Bill.

151. Speech made to the West Midlands Conservative Political Centre in Birmingham, 20 April 1968.

152. Z Layton-Henry, 1984, *op cit* p71.

153. See D Spearman, *New Society*, 9 May 1968.

154. Astonishingly a new authorised biography of Powell by Simon Heffer argues that Powell was not a racialist although there is an acceptance that Powell never withdrew his remarks. Black and Asian people were dismayed at the responses to Powell's death in 1998 when political leaders, including Tony Blair described Powell as a fine statesman.

155. See the debates in the press in mid February 1995.

156. Rose *et al, Colour and Citizenship*, pp551-605.

157. *Ibid* p569.

158. T Benn, *Again the Tide: Diaries 1973-76*, Hutchinson, 1989, entry for 16 January 1974.

159. Z Layton-Henry, 1984, *op cit,* p73.

160. This is what Heath said to the author in November 1997 in an interview for Radio Four.

161. D Smith, *Racial Disadvantage in Britain*, Penguin, 1977.

162. *Hansard*, 4 March 1976, col 1601.

163. Home Office Minister Alex Lyon, *Hansard*, 15 January 1976, oral answers, col 560-561.

164. See *The Politics of The Race Relations Act 1976*, Lord Lester of Herne Hill, Runnymede Trust, 1997.

165. S Saggar *op cit* p117.

166. J Twitchin in *Five Views of Multiracial Britain*, Commission for Racial Equality/BBC, 1978, p6.

167. See T Russel, *The Tory Party: Its Policies, Divisions and Future*, Penguin, 1978.

168. *World in Action*, Granada Television, 30 January 1978.

169. Saggar, p120.

170. Full quote in *The Independent* 20 March 1995.

171. P Dodd, *The Battle Over Britain*, Demos, pp 26-27.

172. For an excellent detailed analysis of this see the section *Racism and Equal Opportunity Policy* in *Racism and Anti-racism* (ed) Peter Braham *et al*, OUP, 1992.

173. Saggar, p193.

174. N Murray, *Anti-racists and Other Demons: The Press and Ideology in Thatcher's Britain*, Institute of Race Relations, Race and Class

Pamphlet, no 12, 1989, pp2-3.

175. For a detailed description of how this happened see Gordon and Klug, *op cit*, 1988.

176. See C Searle, *Your Daily Dose: Racism and the Sun*, Campaign for Press and Broadcasting Freedom, 1989.

177. See Saggar pp129-134.

178. *The Brixton Disorders 10-12 April 1981; Report of an Inquiry*, 1981.

179. C Brown, *Black and White Britain, op cit*, and C Brown and P Gay *Racial Discrimination: 17 years after the Act, op cit*.

180. C Brown, *Black and White Britain*, Heinemann.

181. See the Parliamentary Debates in *Hansard* on the 13 July 1989 and also transcript of BBC1 programme, Hong Kong – a matter of honour, 12 June 1989.

182. The Free Market Case for Immigration, report for Public Eye, BBC2, 1990, and Corry B *et al*, report for *The South China Post*, 1990.

183. For details of the effects of these changes see the report of the Glidewell Panel, 16 April 1996.

184. Conservative Central Office, *Our First Eight Years; The Achievements of the Conservative Government since May 1979*.

185. *The Independent*, 22 November 1995.

186. *Setting the Agenda on Race*, Runnymede Bulletin, September 1998.

187. S Spencer 'The Impact of Immigration on Race Relations', in *Race Relations in Britain (*ed) T Blackstone, B Parekh and P Sanders, 1998, p80.

188. *The Guardian*, 26 February 1996.

189. *The Independent*, 26 October 1995.

190. 9 January 1996.

191. *The New Untouchables: Immigration and the New World Worker*, IB Tauris, 1995, p1.

192. Jowell R *et al* eds, *British Social Attitudes*, the 12th Report, Social and Community Planning Research, 1991.

193. Runnymede Trust/NOP Survey 1991.

194. See for example the MORI survey carried out for CAFOD in November 1995.

195. Hearings took place in February 1996 and details were collated by the Southall Monitoring Group.

196. For an excellent analysis of this see S Spencer 'The Impact of Immigration Policy on Race Relations' in *Race Relations In Britain*, 1998, *op cit.*

197. *Immigration Survey Research Report*, CRE, December 1995.

198. *The Observer* 3 September 1995.

199. Quoted in *The Independent*, 16 November 1995.

200. *The Guardian*, 12 December 1995.

201. For a set of persuasive arguments on this see S Spencer (ed) *Strangers and Citizens*, IPPR/Rivers Oram Press 1994.

202. S Spencer, 'The Impact of Immigration Policy on Race Relations', *op cit.*

203. Hansard, 11 December 1995, col 778.

204. Hansard, 11 December 1995, col 810.

205. Quoted by the Bishop of Liverpool during the House of Lords Committee Debate on the Asylum and Immigration Bill, 23 April 1996.

206. Commons Second Reading debate, 11 December 1995, col 746.

207. UN Committee on the Elimination of Racial Discrimination Report, March 1996.

208. In paper presented to the Royal Geographical Society, 7 January 1997.

209. *'Bogus and phoney': the Representation of Refugees in the UK Media*, Leeds Metropolitan University, April 1996, p15.

210. Statement made in Parliament during the second reading debate on the 1995 Bill, quoted *The Independent*, 12 December 1995.

211. Home Office press release, 159/95.

212. See the report in *The Enfield Advertiser*, 5 August 1998.

213. Report published in 1997.

214. HO Press release, 5 October 1995.

215. Press Release 18 May 1997.

216. M Linton, *Was it the Sun What Did It?* Nuffield College, 30 October 1995, p5.

217. *Ibid*, p5.

218. See the press coverage over the week of 14 February 1995.

219. Personal communication by three press journalists working for three right of centre newspapers.

220. See the debate in *The Telegraph*, 13 February 1995.

221. For a full description of these events look in *The Runnymede Bulletin*, No 291.

222. See *The Evening Standard*, 4 December 1995.

223. *The Guardian*, 5 October 1995.

224. A declaration, *Free Speech and Race Relations in a Democratic Society: Principles of Good Practice and Conduct for Political Campaigners*, CRE, April 1997 signed by all the political party leaders and Brian Mawhinney on behalf of the Conservatives.

225. This series of interviews were carried out in the two months after the election. Some of the key people interviewed had also been interviewed in the lead up to the election.

226. Bernie Grant expressed his anger at the use of the bulldog in *The Evening Standard* 28 April 1997 as did Darcus Howe in *The Daily Telegraph* 18 April 1997.

227. Meeting held in April 1998.

228. Reported in *The Guardian*, 12 November 1998.

229. Second Reading of the 1995 Asylum and Immigration in the House of Lords, 14 March, 1996, col 966.

230 Keynote speech made at CRE conference on The Future of Race Relations, 4 July 1994, p11.

231. 29 January 1997, p1.

232. Speech made in Calcutta to The Confederation of Indian Industry, 9 January 1997, p6.

233. Reported in *The Gujarat Samachar*, 7 March 1997.

234. 2 July 1995, p2.

235. 20 August 1995 p2.

236. Speech made at Westminster House 12 May 1998.

237. See the well-documented cases in various publications by the Joint Council for the Welfare of Immigrants.

238. Speech made on 18 January 1997.

239. In *The Guardian* 13 January 1997.

240. NOP/Opinion Leader Research/surveys carried out for the IPPR and published 5 February 1997.

241. In an unpublished interview with the author, 30 May 1995.

242. 'Do We Need People Like Michael Howard?' 27 May 1995.

CHAPTER 4

243. For a detailed account of how this is being done, see *One America in the 21st Century: Forging a New Future, The President's Initiative on Race,* October 1998.

244. *Routes of Racism,* Trentham Books, 1996, p40.

245. Annual Report, Canadian Anti-Racism Education and Research Society, p6.

246. There have been many cases of alleged and proven discriminatory practices among the Canadian police force and the judiciary. The target groups are either Native Canadians or blacks. See for example, G York, *Judicial Reform: Manitoba Natives tell their story.*

247. M Cannon, *The Invisible Empire, Racism in Canada,* Random House, 1995, p126.

248. For a comprehensive account of this see M Cannon, *China Tide, The Revealing Story of the Hong Kong Exodus to Canada,* Harper Collins, 1989.

249. An internal report by the Department of Immigration and Citizenship tracked public attitudes towards immigrants from 1975-1985 which shows significant shifts which are related too wider concerns about unemployment etc. An attitudes survey by Multiculturalism and Citizenship in 1991 showed that on the whole Canadians felt less comfortable with Indo-Pakistanis, Sikhs, Arabs and Muslims than with most other groups.

250. This information was communicated to the author during the extensive interviews within the Department of Multiculturalism and Citizenship in Ottawa in 1995.

251. Annual Report 1992/93, Department of Citizenship and Immigration, pii.

252. Annual Report, Multiculturalism and Citizenship, 1998 p2.

253. Annual Report, Multiculturalism and Citizenship, 1989/90 p3.

254. *Ibid.,* pviii.

255 See the Annual Report, *Operation of the Canadian Multicultural Act,* 1992/93, p1

256. Annual Report, Department of Citizenship and Immigration 1994, p1.

257. See Y Alibhai-Brown, 'Bring England in From the Cold', in *New Statesman,* 11 July 1997.

258. *Economic and Social Impacts of Immigration,* 1991, chapter 9.

259. *Ibid* p135.

260. *National Survey into Multicultualism and Canadians*, Multicultural and Citizenship Department, 1991.

261. Speaking at the IPPR seminar on 26 October 1996.

262. See the Annual Consultation Reports, Department of Citizenship and Immigration, 1995.

263. Minderhedennota, government document on the ethnic minorities, 1982, The Hague, *Staattsitgeveri en Drukkeriji* p5.

264. Paper by the Home Office Minister presented to Parliament on the 27 March 1992.

265. G Verbeck, P Sceepers, and F Wester, *Attitudes Towards Ethnic Minorities*, paper presented at the Unversity of Bristol, 1-4 April 1995.

266. CSCE Human Dimension Seminar, Case Studies on National Minorities Issues, positive results, May 1993, p4.

267. Personal communication, government official in The Hague, May 1996.

268. This was confirmed by a number of independent voluntary organisations who monitor the role of government in these areas. ADO is one of them.

269. Personal communcation, Berlin, May 1996.

270. See C Wilpert, 'The Idealogical and Institutional Foundations of Racism in Germany' in *Racism and Migration in Western Europe*, J Solomos and J Wrench (eds), Oxford 1993.

271. *The Quest for Anti-Discrimination Policies to Protect Migrants in Germany; An assessment of the political discussion and proposal for legislation*. Draft paper, January 1997, p2.

272. See IPPR, *Immigration as an Economic Asset*, ed S Spencer, 1994, Trentham Books.

273. Reported in *The Guardian*, 5 March 1997.

274. Germany: an undeclared immigration country, *New Community*, 21: p19.

275. 'Germany: Nationalism, Nazism and Violence' in *Racist Violence in Europe*, T Bjorgo and R Witte (ed) St Martin's Press, 1993, p159.

276. *MultiKulturelles Berlin*, M.Lorbeer (ed) Elfanten Press, pp8-9.

277. Steven Vertovec, Berlin Multikulti: Germany, 'foreigners' and 'world openness', draft paper, 1996, endnote 30.

278. Personal communication.

279. In *Multicultural Strategies in the Federal Republic of Germany,* Paper for the Nordic Migration Conference, Esbjerg.

280. Personal communication, May 1996.

281. Personal communications, cited by Vertovec *op cit.*

282. Interview with five such groups in Berlin and elsewhere, showed that this is an accurate reflection of how many felt.

283. Personal communication, June 1996.

284. I am indebted to Sarah Spencer for her analysis of this. See her 'The Impact of Immigration Policies on Race Relations', in *Race Relations in Britain,* 1998, *op cit.*

285. Figure quoted by John Major in his speech in India, reported in *The Guardian,* 10 January 1997.

286. Speech made 2 July 1998.

287. Personal communication, representatives from the Chamber of Commerce, Keith Vaz MP and white local councillors in May 1996.

288. Home Office Research Study 176, 1997.

289. Press release no.629, CRE, 5 January 1997.

290. *New Statesman,* 13 December 1996.

291. S Spencer, 1998, *op cit,* p89.

292. See for example the annual report of the Canadian Department of Multiculturalim 1996-97.

293. *The Guardian* 21 May 1997.

294. *Roots of the Future, op cit.*

295. See *Britain, Renewing our Identity,* Mark Leonard, p57.

296. *Ibid*

297. See Dr Rae Sibbitt, 1997, *op cit.*

298. *Islamaphobia, A Challenge For us All,* 1997.

299. An IPPR seminar on Young Muslims revealed how alienated this group felt and how this was leading to what one Muslim newspaper editor described as a 'British Intifada'. In his interview on an Asian programme on BBC2 with the other political leaders, John Major made a powerful statement about the perceptions of Muslims in Britain. This is still remembered by many Muslims.

300. Foreign and Commonwealth Office, *Facts and Fairytales Revisited,* June 1995.

301. In May 1998 Jack Straw set up a Race Forum consisting of black and Asian Britons from various walks of life. The idea is that the Forum will work with the Home Secretary and exert some kind of influence at the heart of the government.

302. At the IPPR seminar on community conflicts held in February 1998, this was a point raised by ethnic minority opinion makers like Gurbux Singh, the Chief Executive of Haringey.

303. Gieseck, V Heilemann, and H von Loeffelholz, *Economic and Social Implications of Migration into the FR of Germany*, paper at IPPR seminar 6-7 March 1994.

304. Julian Simons, *Immigration the Demographic and Economic Facts*, Cato Institute, 1995.

305. See Colin Brown and Jean Lawton, *Illicit Drug use in Portsmouth and Havant*, Policy Studies Institute, 1998 p88.

306. Personal Communication, with a press officer at the Department of Transport, May 1998.

307. Personal Communications with a key member of the Campaigns section at the CRE, August 1996.

308. See the evaluation of this by CRE Research in August 1994.

309. For the two evaluations see *Evaluation of Edinburgh District Council's Zero Tolerance Campaign*, Jenny Kitzinger and Kate Hunt, Glasgow Media Group, Edinburgh District Council Women's Committee, 1993 and *Zero Tolerance Campaign Evaluation Report July 1995*, Market Research Group, UK, Aberdeen July 1995.

310. A Vrij *et al*, *Reducing Ethnic Prejudice through Public Communication Programmes*, Paper given at the University of Southampton, 19 January 1996

311. See Mark Leonard, *op cit* pp46-47.

312. The BBC2 documentary programmes on how the Treasury informs and influences the media showed just how effective and sophisticated the machinery is.

313. Personal Communication with a senior Home Office official, November 1997.

314. Press release, CRE, 14 June 1995.